Theology in Music

How Christian Themes Permeate Classic Songs

Kenneth Francis

En Route Books and Media, LLC

Saint Louis, MO

USA

⊕*ENROUTE*
Make the time

En Route Books and Media, LLC
5705 Rhodes Avenue
St. Louis, MO 63109

Cover credit: Sebastian Mahfood

Library of Congress Control Number: 2026933322

Editor's Note: The following chapters, some updated, first appeared in *New English Review*: Chapter 1, July 2020; Chapter 2, May 2019; Chapter 3, Feb 2024; Chapter 4, Jan 2018; Chapter 5, Sept 2023; Chapter 6, Nov 2022; Chapter 9, June 2023; Chapter 10, May 2024.

Table of Contents

Introduction

This book does not focus on themes in faith-based music or hymns, but instead it deconstructs the hidden grammar in classic popular songs theologically marinated in existential narratives, featuring idolatry, sin, love, pathos, and meaning. And what better religion to focus on than Christianity for such themes, from the soul-music classics of the 1960/70s, to the Top 100 Billboard hits of the same eras.

Christianity is a metaphorical umbrella, under which lies a multiple ensemble of ribs (Genesis 2:21-22). These reach into and establish spiritual concepts and emotions encompassing the roots and culture of mostly Western civilisation and beyond, whether it be pro- or anti-Christianity. Thus, Christianity's profound grip on Mankind is unescapable.

We see this first-hand in the existential plight of homo sapiens, whose lives' (intermittently) experiences mirror that of a crucified Christ atop of Mount Calvary. It permeates our dreams, desires, and quest for meaning in life. No other religion touches the human spirit quite like Christianity, that promises those, who are redeemed, an afterlife of bliss beyond the grave. For Christians, it is the glue that holds us together, just like the cross-shaped molecule, the laminin, the fingerprints of our Creator, written across our hearts, which is a vital biological protein for our existence by holding us together.

Many artists worldwide get their inspiration from Christianity, especially in music. On Naturalism, there is no inspiration. On such a world view, the Walker Brothers' song "The Sun Ain't Gonna Shine Anymore," is reduced to the Godless title of, "The Nuclear Fusion Ain't Gonna Radiate Light Anymore." Doesn't have the same ring to it, does it? Especially when it's been screeched by a hairless ape hard-wired to electro chemicals in the brain, according to the hidden grammar of Darwinian theory, with no disrespect to the wonderful creatures of the Animal Kingdom. In a nutshell: The Bible tells us that humans are made in God's image (Genesis 1:26-28).

The singer/songwriter, Nick Cave, regularly reads the Bible. He once said in his recorded lectures that any true love song is a song for God and ascribed the mellowing of his music to a shift in focus from the Old Testament to the New Testament.

When asked if he had interest in religions outside of Christianity, Cave said that he had a passing, sceptical interest but was a "hammer-and-nails kind of guy." Even the idiom, "nailed it," with its sentiments of The Crucifixion, refers to a Truth (Logos) statement or something done perfectly. Despite this, Cave remains vague about his true belief or nonbelief in existence of God.

There are lots of other famous singers like Cave, as their music has one thing in common with the Australian singer: A Christian tapestry is woven into the themes of their songs, whether they be about love, hate, suffering, joy, happiness, loneliness, heartbreak, grief, guilt, remorse, or righteous indignation, good, evil, Heaven or Hell. Even the Prince of Darkness is an entity in Christianity.

Bob Dylan, at one point in his career, became a Christian, but it is unclear what his beliefs are now. In an interview on *60 Minutes* in 2004 with Ed Bradley, Dylan said why he doesn't retire is because he made a deal to "get where I am now." He added: "It all goes back to the destiny thing. I made a bargain with it a long time ago, and I'm holding up my end." When asked who he made a deal with, Dylan said: "With the Chief Commander of this earth and the world we can't see." This must be the devil, because God does not make bargain pacts. But it's not just Dylan alluding to some kind of Faustian Pact. Many contemporary pop stars say similar things while being intervened, not to mention their stage performance marinated in Satanism.

In the music industry, many, if not all, songwriters are unwitting theologians of one kind or another. If Christ Jesus is The Logos, then there is no escaping the logic in the narrative, even if violating it, when expressing themes in music, film, theatre, literature, and many other genres in the Arts. Testament to this are the lyrics in the songs of Johnny Cash, Elvis Presley, Ray Charles, Al Green, Van Morrison, and a vast host of the world's biggest music male and female stars of the 20th century. And it's the 20th century on which I'll focus in this book because, in general, in my opinion, there have been no classic songs post-1980s. In the 1970s, an era of wonderful music, one of the greatest love songs of all time, "Me and Mrs Jones," was released in '72. It is a song about the odd diversity of misery and joy, while breaking of the Seventh Commandment.

Even the Rolling Stones' "Sympathy for the Devil" is steeped in Christian themes, acknowledging the existence of the devil and the crucifixion of Jesus.

As for the existence of the 'Chief Commander in the world we cannot see': The band Queen's monster classic hit back in 1975, was "Bohemian Rhapsody", a song marinated in theological themes. There are many theories about the meaning of this song, but one of them is quite interesting: It served as Freddie Mercury's way of coming out as a homosexual.

According to an article in *Genius,* quoting Mercury's biographer Lesley-Ann Jones, who was allegedly told by Freddie's lover Jim Hutton: "'Bohemian Rhapsody' *was* Freddie's confessional," Hutton told Jones. "It was about how different his life could have been, and how much happier he might have been, had he just been able to be himself, the whole of his life."

Think about it: Could the first verse represent Mercury metaphorically killing his old self ('Mama, just killed a man')? Later in the song, the lyrics question reality, the struggle against good and evil, looking up to the sky for inspiration from God, while rebelling against God, the abandonment of the soul, gilt, pathos, and Beelzebub.

Speaking in Germany in 1985, Mercury joked about his own death, in footage for a documentary, called *The Show Must Go On: The Queen + Adam Lambert Story*. Regarding his death and if he would like to go to Heaven, he said: "No, I don't want to. Hell is much better. Look at the interesting people you are going to meet down there."

"Bohemian Rapsody" fades out with the following lyrics:

"Nothing really matters to me
Any way the wind blows."

Mercury died of Aids-related complications in 1991.

The old saying, 'Be careful what you wish for' comes to mind. Say a prayer that this gifted musician made his peace with God and is in a better place.

Another gay icon is the Pet Shop Boys' lead singer, Neil Tennant. In his 1987 song co-written with Chris Lowe, "It's a Sin," Tennant laments on his time at the Catholic St Cuthbert's High School in

Newcastle upon Tyne. He ended up feeling that everything he had done or was going to do was a sin. Consider the following lyrics, with much emotional sentiments (who isn't a sinner?):

When I look back upon my life
It's always with a sense of shame
I've always been the one to blame
For everything I long to do
No matter when or where or who
Has one thing in common, too

[Chorus]
It's a, it's a, it's a, it's a sin
It's a sin
Everything I've ever done
Everything I ever do
Every place I've ever been
Everywhere I'm going to
It's a sin

Billy Joel, who is not gay, sang about rejecting Heaven and the saints in his song "Only the Good Die Young." The song's protagonist is a teenager who has a crush on a Catholic girl, but she refuses his advances. Some radio stations tried to ban or censor the song because of its anti-Catholic content:

You Catholic girls start much too late,
But sooner or later it comes down to fate
I might as well be the one…
…They say there's a Heaven for those who will
      wait
Some say it's better, but I say it ain't
I'd rather laugh with the sinners than cry with
      the saints
The sinners are much more fun
You know that only the good die young.

There are echoes of Milton's *Paradise Lost* in the lyrics in that it is better to reign in Hell than to serve in Heaven. According to Joel, the minute they banned the song, the album featuring it, *The Stranger* (1977), started shooting up the charts. In a 2008 interview, Joel also pointed out one part of the lyrics that nearly all the song's critics missed – the boy in the song failed to have sex or a relationship with the girl; thus, she kept her chastity.

Welcome to the world of classic songs permeated with Christian themes.

Chapter 1

Idolatry and Sin in Love Songs

Human history is the long terrible story of Man trying to find something other than God which will make him happy.—C.S. Lewis

With the word 'Sin' in the title of this chapter, I'm assuming it will only appeal to my Christian readers. But I'm also hoping that people of other faiths or world views might ponder or agree with this message. There's nothing like a little gentle persuasion in spreading the Word (Logos), even if it puts 'a stone in someone's shoe.' And C.S. Lewis, metaphorically, certainly put a lot of stones in a lot of shoes.

To begin, many music lovers might not be aware that some of the words in the greatest love songs ever written are infused with idolatry. I'm not referring to standard love songs void of worshiping the love interest of a man or woman. It's when they deify their subjects of desire, I believe that in certain cases criticism is justified.

9

Some love lyrics are intentionally idolatrous while others are innocently written with a passion to create a beautiful song. There are also lyrics that are blatantly vulgar or sinful. Unfortunately, for the devout Christian, many of these songs are classics. One of my all-time *guilty* pleasures, in the real meaning of the adjective, is 'Me and Mrs Jones,' a stunningly seductive love song about adultery, sung in 1972 by the late, great soul-singer, Billy Paul.

In the *Financial Times* (April 17, 2015), Ludovic Hunter-Tilney wrote: "'Me and Mrs Jones, we got a thing going on,' Paul sang in a beautifully sultry tone. 'We both know that it's wrong, but it's much too strong to let it go now.' Tinkling piano, strings and a sighing saxophone made the extramarital liaison sound the very height of sophistication. Never has the Seventh Commandment been broken so smoothly."

As for the music industry that regularly breaks the First Commandment: One would have to be incredibly naïve or blind to not notice how diabolically possessed this hellhole of debauchery has become. Almost every gig or music video is accompanied by satanic symbolism and raw sexual exhibitionism. It's difficult to know when exactly this began, but

The Beatles were a good candidate for the musical 'Big Bang' that set the ball rolling and created some dark elements amongst fellow musicians and fans that, over a span of almost 60 years, has continued to this day.

Whether these bands were created psy-ops is unclear, but many conspiracy theorists, whose past predictions have almost all come true, believe lots of groups *were* manufactured to brainwash their fans in order to break-up the nuclear family, emasculate men, sexualise society, and breed disdain for Christianity; the perfect agenda for State control over the dumbed-down masses singing along to 'Sympathy for the Devil' and 'Losing My Religion.'

As for the Beatles' lyrics in the albums that followed *Rubber Soul* in the early to mid-1960s, such music continued the journey down the secular 'rabbit hole,' combined with morally good lyrics to keep their image wholesome by sugar-coating the negative content. For example: The Godless 'Eleanor Rigby's' lyrics say, "no one can save, all the lonely people." Really? Not even Christ? What a dire, hopeless line of despair to include in a song.

Then, by 1968 on *The Beatles* 'white' album, McCartney sang: 'Why don't we do it in the road?'

Within five years, The Beatles went from 'I Want to Hold Your Hand,' to why don't we have sex on the road, as "nobody will be watching us"? Raw 'noble-savage' sentiments much closer to animal behaviour than civilized Man with respect for God.

Regarding disrespect for God, let's not forget the lyrics in Elton John's 1971 classic hit, 'Tiny Dancer': "… Jesus freaks out on the street/Handing tickets out for God." At the time of its release, some radio stations banned this song due to the blasphemous opening lines of the second verse, written by Elton John's lyricist, Bernie Taupin.

But it's not only blatantly blasphemous lyrics in songs. Some lyrics or symbolism, possibly innocuous, slip through the net of our consciousness. (As an aside: Most of us are familiar with the ubiquitous one-eye Pagan imagery in the pop industry, which goes back decades. Such early examples can be seen, amongst many other groups, on some Beatles, Walker Brothers, and Doors' album covers. Today, it's everywhere.

It's difficult to fully ascertain what the one-eye represents in the music industry, as there are many meanings for it from ancient times. Some close observers of cults believe when you hide one eye, you effectively block half of your vision. They believe that, in symbolic terms, you become half-blind to the truth. By hiding one eye, celebrities symbolically 'sacrifice' a vital part of their being for temporary material gain, thus, 'selling their soul.' Whether this is true or not, it's certainly the subject of an entire essay.)

But back to lyrics: Frontman singer of The Walker Brothers, the late Scott Walker, was a humble but enigmatic recluse who wrote and produced very disturbing, avant-garde material when he left the group. But I want to focus on a song, from a purely theological perspective, that he sang in 1966 while with the 'Brothers': 'The Sun Ain't Gonna Shine Anymore.'

This song is a popular music masterpiece, one of the greatest love songs of all time. It is about a man who is spellbound by an ex-lover. However, and this is where idolatry creeps in, he elevates this woman to the status of a goddess. He implies that, without her, he's going to commit suicide ("… I can't go on …"). Really? Not even Christ can save him? His fixation and craving for this woman have blinded him spiritually, when his priority should be his primary relationship with Jesus, because with Him, you'll never be "without love."

But the life of the lonely character of this song, outside of pursuing his Ex, is empty ("Emptiness is a place you're in"). And she has the power to meta-phorically cloud his tearful vision from the sun and stop the moon from rising in the sky (I thought only God could do that).

See how subtle and powerful the lyrics are, ripe for entering the subconsciouses listener's mind? And the fact that the song has an incredible melody, sung by a teen pop icon with an amazing voice, makes it all the more seductive. As for the lyri-cist/composer(s): No disrespect to the talented duo Bob Crewe and Bob Gaudio, as it's unlikely idolatry lyrics were on their minds when they crafted this sumptuous number-one hit during the cusp of the 'Summer of Love.'

But theological interpretations aside: What about the atheist who says such dramatic love songs can be secularist and don't need to prioritise God before the human love interest? In that case, the secularist must be consistent with his Naturalistic, non-theistic world view.

In such a world, Naturalism can't present an adequate account of love. Scientifically/biologically, such behaviour is the result of atoms bumping into one another in the brain of an evolved, hairless ape. And what ape would crave another creature's affections—or sing about them so passionately, for that matter? According to atheism, sensory experiences to the brain aren't "about" anything; they're just input/output circuits. There are no "thoughts about love," thus, poignant lamentations in the mind are illusory.

It seems the atheist would be bereft of any phenomenological meaning (the method by which the observer examines the data without trying to provide an explanation of them). He would be at the mercy of the raw physical material of the universe as perceived through microscopes, telescopes, and laboratory chemical observations: A great organised network of numerous molecules in motion, enzymes, and massive objects and spheres orbiting stars.

More: This is where it gets bizarre, if God's creation is reduced to Darwinian, Naturalistic grammar: The lyrics of the song's chorus would read something like this: *"The nuclear fusion ain't' gonna radi-*

ate light anymore/The earth's natural satellite ain't gonna rise in the celestial sphere/The secreted liquid from lacrimal glands are always aerosoling your visual organs/When you're without a chemical reaction in the brain."

Doesn't have the same romantic ring to it, does it? See original lyrics below in brackets.

> (*The sun ain't gonna shine anymore*
> *The moon ain't gonna rise in the sky*
> *The tears are always clouding your eyes*
> *When you're without love*)

In an interview with LifeSiteNews (June 17), Archbishop Vigano said: "… What has the much-celebrated movement of Romanticism taught us, if not that reason must yield to feeling and that the will cannot govern the passions, that 'the heart is not commanded,' while in fact the opposite is true?"

Maybe I'm over-analysing all this and sometimes a 'cigar is just a cigar,' but one can't deny the lyrics are focused *primarily* and *exclusively* on the love of a flawed, sinful, imperfect human, and not on love for a perfect God. It's almost like this wreck of a jilted man's soul can only be saved through the

love of his former girlfriend. His extreme idealisa-
tion of her has emasculated him and made him
weak. But his desperation is nothing compared to
the love interest in Barry Ryan's 1968 hit-song
'Eloise':

You know I'm on my knees yeh
I said please
You're all I want, so hear my prayer
My prayer
My Eloise is like the stars that please the night
The sun that makes the day
That lights the way
And when the star goes by
I hold it in my hands and cry
Her love was mine
You know my sun will shine.

If you replace the word 'Eloise' in this song with
'God', it makes more sense. But it's not just sad,
desperate men who crave the ultimate love of wom-
en in these over-dramatic love songs. Consider this
lady below who would be better off being a follower
of Christ instead of a fallen man. In 1963, Little
Peggy March sang, "I Will Follow Him":

I will follow him, follow him
Wherever he may go,
And near him,
I always will be,
For nothing can keep me away,
He is my destiny . . .
I love him, I love him, I love him,
And where he goes, I'll follow, I'll follow, I'll fol-
    low.

According to the Bible, worshiping Man before God is not compatible with Christianity: 'Who changed the truth of God into a lie, and worshiped and served the creature more than the Creator, who is blessed forever. Amen.' (Romans: KJ Bible)

That's not to say all love songs should be about God but consider the power and beauty of the lyrics in the hymn 'Oh Holy Night.' This song could never refer to a human being, as it would sound delusionary, over-the-top worship-mania. But when referring to God, it makes so much sense. The same goes for most, if not all, Christian hymns. And it's not just Christians like me who feel this way about certain love lyrics that border on idolatry and broken, worldly dreams.

The late rock-star, Frank Zappa, who was no friend of Christianity, said the following about romantic love lyrics: "I detest love lyrics. I think one of the causes of bad mental health in the United States is that people have been raised on 'love lyrics.' You're a young kid and you hear all those 'love lyrics,' right? Your parents aren't telling you the truth about love, and you can't really learn about it in school. You're getting the bulk of your 'behaviour norms' mapped out for you in the lyrics to some dumb f*****g love song. It's a subconscious training that creates desire for an imaginary situation which will never exist for you. People who buy into that mythology go through life feeling that they got cheated out of something."

A lot of what Zappa says is true. Although love for one another is a good thing if it's Holy, for many it's driven by carnal lust and possession of the other person. Worldly love is also finite, but the love of God is eternal.

Some of the greatest love songs don't deify the love interest in the lyrics or even mention the word love; I'm thinking here about songs like Clifford T Ward's poignant 'Home Thoughts From Abroad': A song about a breezy, romantic chap who, in the form of writing a letter, expresses how he misses his ex-girlfriend. Also, in another example, "Morning Has Broken," written by Christian author Eleanor Farjeon, and sung in the 1970s by Cat Stevens (now known as Yusef Islam). If you listen to this beautiful song, you'll find it hard not to be elevated to a higher place. And the word 'love' is not mentioned throughout the entire song. It is simply a song about *praising* the gifts God gave us but not idolizing them.

Chapter 2

The Beatles and the Dark Side of the Road

In the first verse of his poem, Annus Mirabilis, Philip Larkin writes: 'Sexual intercourse began/In nineteen sixty-three (which was rather late for me)—Between the end of the Chatterley ban/ And the Beatles' first LP.'

It was always assumed The Beatles were the "good guys," while The Rolling Stones were the "bad guys," the latter being the type of rocker-rogues that parents wouldn't want their daughter dating. Unlike the Stones, the loveable, boyish Beatles seemed to have started out wholesome, but they gradually began to write vulgar, blasphemous songs without many fans noticing it.

In an interview with John Lennon, conducted around the time of the band's breakup (1970), Lennon said: "Things are left out, about what bastards we were . . . You have to be a bastard to make it. That's a fact. And The Beatles were the biggest bastards on Earth." (The quote resurfaced in Philip Norman's biography, *John Lennon: The Life.*)

But when John, Paul, George and Ringo started to become popular worldwide in the early Sixties, they certainly didn't come across as bastards. And their songs were all about 'clean' courtship between men and women. Songs like "She Loves You," "I Want to Hold Your Hand," and "Love Me Do" paid homage to romantic innocence in the relatively simple lives of teenagers and young adults in love.

But the lyrics and mood in their music changed incrementally from album to album. Paradoxically, this moral decline in the lyrics of some of their songs resulted in, for many including myself, better and more creative music.

As mentioned above, their first few albums were all about love and happiness. However, their 1965 albums *Help* and *Rubber Soul* were a turning point for the band in terms of lyrics. The new wave of songs by the Fab Four alluded to existential confusion and troubled relationships and contained cynically pessimistic lyrics not heard of in their earlier stuff. Songs like "Help!" "You've Got To Hide Your Love Away," and "I'm Looking Through You" were nothing like the starry-eyed, optimistic ditties of earlier years.

It's also interesting to note that 1965 was a year that saw a major societal upheaval in the West that led to the Sexual Revolution. Despite this socially negative cultural shift, the top 100 hits of '65 were arguably the greatest songs ever written and composed in pop history.

In America, heralding in the year at Number One, was, portentously, "The Eve of Destruction," sung by Barry McGuire; The Bible says: 'For they have sown the wind, and they shall reap the whirlwind' (Hosea 8:7): The Palm Sunday Tornado Outbreak on April 13 resulted in an estimated 47 tornadoes in six Midwestern states with fatalities in the hundreds and millions of dollars' worth of damage; Bob Dylan was called 'Judas,' after he went electric in '65; cannabis and LSD—used irresponsibly and recklessly—became popular recreational drugs; the beginning of the US health-costs crisis and 'Great Society' for black people, the latter (launched by Democrat, Lyndon Johnson) replacing the pay cheque with the welfare cheque; the breaking of the movie code with the first cinematic screening of female breasts in mainstream films like *The Pawnbroker* and *Repulsion* by Roman Polanski, a "sexually repressed" female virgin's dreams lead to two murders.

More: the culmination of Vatican 2 and the seemingly hijacked Catholic Church's distorted teachings erring on dogma, thus, loss of power over decadent Hollywood; unbridled promiscuity and the Pill; British theatre critic, Kenneth Tynan, was the first person to say "fuck" during a talk on a BBC programme; and if the "best music is played in Hell," then The Beatles' hits of the mid- to late-'60s were unfortunately testament to that metaphorical adage, if Lennon/McCartney and Harrison really wrote and composed those songs. There is much speculation amongst conspiracy theorists hypothesising that the sophistication of Beatles' song lyrics and composition were way above the intellect of four young lads aged in their 20s from Liverpool, with such songs being way above their life experiences.

Names like musicologist Theodor Adorno, who died in 1969 shortly before the break-up of The Beatles, as well as other music geniuses from the Tavistock Institute who are mentioned as possible composer/song-writers. Beatles researcher Mike

Williams makes a compelling case for this in his four-hour podcast.

I'll let the reader decide for himself/herself if such a theory holds water, as I remain agnostic on this and many other things I was told to be fact during my early life and beyond. Nearly all the things that conspiracy theorists warned us about since the death of JFK turned out to be spoiler alerts.

But back to The Beatles. According to John Lennon during the mid-'60s, "we're more popular than Jesus now." What Lennon probably meant was only those with plastic or rubber souls viewed the Fab Four more popular than Jesus.

Lennon said: "Christianity will go. It will vanish and shrink. I needn't argue about that; I'm right and I'll be proved right. We're more popular than Jesus now; I don't know which will go first—rock 'n' roll or Christianity. Jesus was all right but his disciples were thick and ordinary. It's them twisting it that ruins it for me." (The only 'twisted' disciple was Judas.)

But back to the impressive LP, *Rubber Soul,* and the albums that succeeded it: Mature, but cold, transient sexual encounters are the curious lyrics of the classic "Norwegian Wood," with a possible reference/interpretation to arson, in revenge for being made to 'sleep in the bath;' while "Think For Yourself" was snarky and pointed to the 'good riddance' of the break-up of a relationship.

The lyrics in the albums that followed *Rubber Soul* continued the journey into the dark side, combined with morally good lyrics to keep their image 'clean'. The Godless Eleanor Rigby's lyrics say, "no one can save, all the lonely people" Really? Not even Jesus Christ?

However, by 1968 on The Beatles 'white' album, McCartney's lyrics moved to the darkest side of the road. The song?: "Why Don't We Do It In the Road." Think about this for a moment: Within five years, The Beatles went from "I Want to Hold Your Hand," to "Why Don't We F**k On Some Roadway," as "nobody will be watching us." Even the philosopher Jean-Jacques Rousseau would wince in his grave on hearing the situation ethic of such 'noble' savage sentiments.

In his book *Many Years From Now*, Barry Miles quotes McCartney saying he wrote the above song while on retreat in Rishikesh, India. He saw two monkeys copulating in the street and was impressed at the simplicity of the scene, when compared to the emotional turmoil of human relationships.

McCartney said a male monkey just hopped on the back of this female and "gave her one." He added: "Within two or three seconds he hopped off again and looked around as if to say 'It wasn't me!' and she looked around as if there'd been some mild disturbance . . . And I thought . . . that's how simple the act of procreation is . . . We have horrendous problems with it, and yet animals don't." Animals are not human or moral agents. The monkey forcibly copulated with the female. For a human male to do likewise is rape, a moral abomination.

Friedrich Nietzsche would call this moral inversion the transvaluation of values. So, sorry, Paul, but not sorry: Give me the 'horrendous problems' of human relationships any day instead of 'doing it in the road.'

Other songs on the 'white' album were about borderline suicide ("Yer Blues"); a pervert looking upskirt with mirrors on his booths ("Happiness is a Warm Gun," a master stroke in double entendre, with the phallic metaphors of 'warm gun' [penis], 'bang, bang', [copulation] 'shoot, shoot' [ejaculation], etc), climaxing in the lyrics 'I feel my hand on your trigger.'

During the year when the 'white' album came out, the cult leader Charles Manson, whose followers committed nine murders, said he was inspired by some of these songs. The Manson case is shrouded in conspiracy and mystery, the subject of an entire book to uncover any unresolved theories.

Another twisted song on The Beatles' last album, *Abbey Road*, arguably the greatest LP of all time, was "Maxwell's Silver Hammer." This catchy tune was about a serial killer who hits his victims over the head with a hammer. Once again: From being held lovingly by the hand and 'she loves you' (yea, yea, yea!) to having your brains bashed out with a silver hammer, The Beatles came a long way from the innocent bubble-gum hits of the early days. There are many more songs with questionable meaning in the lyrics, but I've just mentioned a selected few.

However, love them or hate them, from the bright side of their music to the dark side, there will never be a group quite like the Fab Four. Testament to this is what I regard as the greatest song of all time, "A Day in the Life." The song comes from the

1967 album, *Sgt Pepper's Lonely Hearts Club Band* and was banned by the then-BBC because of the 'obscene' lyrics, 'I'd love to turn you on' or drug-dreaming reference, 'had a smoke (cannabis?), and somebody spoke and I went into a dream.' However, the virtuosity of the melody, and intermittent, tremendous build-up of the 41-piece orchestra into chaos, culminating in the most dramatic crescendo in popular music history, is astonishing. For many Beatles' fans and famous musicians, there is no song equal or better than "A Day in the Life."

The beginning of the song was based on stories that Lennon read in a newspaper about Tara Browne, the Guinness heir, dying when he crashed his car into a van; another article in a newspaper referred to surveyors counting 4,000 holes on roads in Blackburn, Lancashire.

Lennon altered the Tara Browne story: 'He blew his mind out in the car' and made the pothole story about filling seats in the Albert Hall (putting 'bums on seats'). Could such a classic song like this be written today, or is modern technology destroying musicians' ability to compose and write such music?

There is also something of Nietzsche's 'Last Man' about the song. Think about it: We live in a world of hi-tech corporate clones who are proxy justice warriors for the State. Many of these people are unwilling to take risks, and they're docile, glued to their tech devices, keeping warm; the days in their lives spent living in the co-work, safe spaces of Silicon Valley.

When the then lead singer of The Byrds, David Crosby, attended the recording of "Day in the Life," he recalled his reaction to hearing the completed song: "Man, I was a dish-rag. I was floored. It took me several minutes to be able to talk after that."

Chapter 3

Dark Music Tones and Voodoo Beats

The key eras when the 'greatest' popular songs topped the music charts were the 1960s to the end of the 1970s. But 'greatest' does not always mean morally good or sacred. We often speak about 'great wars' but there was certainly nothing great about them.

Many culture observers throughout those two eras often comment on the dark side of music and speculate on possible psy-ops elements to create unrest and chaos amongst the Boomer generations and beyond. To doubt this is gullible because the persuasive circumstantial evidence is all around us, and not just in the music industry of yore and now, but in many aspects of contemporary life, particularly geopolitical, upon which I'll briefly touch.

Today, is there a sane person who is proud of and content with the government who rules over him or her? Are some of us so blind and deaf when the elites tell us of their dark tyrannical intentions in advance ('Revelation of the Method') while taking

31

the lack of resistance as implied consent ("You will own nothing, eat bugs, and be happy")? And does it bother any worker that they are being taxed out of existence and treated as second-class citizens in their own country? If you believe that the brand of democracy you are receiving is morally good and not metaphorically gang rape of the mind, then feel free to ignore the 'red-pilled' musings of this humble lay-theologian.

I believe that it is no coincidence that when the Boomers reached adulthood in the mid-1960s, they looked like they were well-socially-engineered indoctrinated model citizens who unwittingly obeyed the diktats of the State, despite causing some civil unrest (possible staged protests) that was advantageous to the State: Problem, reaction, solution.

If the Boomer "scruffy/lazy" hippies thought they were rebellious and against 'The Man' during Woodstock in 1969, as over 460,000 revellers lay in the sun getting stoned and running around naked, they were greatly mistaken. Instead, they unwittingly played into the hands of 'The Man' by being distracted en masse and lost in the blindness of their disordered passions, unaware of the misdirection propaganda from a semi-controlled mainstream media (compared to today, it was a ministry of truth).

Yes, the 1960s was a key epoch for ushering in massive social upheaval, mass hysteria (Beatlemania, etc.) and herd behaviour against the once-traditional Western culture of Christendom. The result? An anti-culture which has culminated today, where tampon dispensers are installed in the men's toilets of the Irish House of Parliament.

The situation in Canada is worse. According to the New York Post: "Tampons and sanitary napkins are now available in men's bathrooms at the Canadian Parliament under a new policy from Prime Minister Justin Trudeau that requires all federally regulated employers—including airports and military bases—to offer free menstrual products in all washrooms, regardless of gender noted on the door."

But back to 1965, the year the Second Vatican Council concluded and right-on nuns and priests started singing "Kumbaya." It was also the date when the Number One hit song that heralded in the year was Barry McGuire's portentous, aptly-titled "Eve of Destruction," written by PF Sloan; a year that saw the birth of the Sexual Revolution, two years before the 'Summer of Love.'

However, one such observer, who sceptically reflected on the music industry of the Sixties and Seventies, was the American researcher David McGowan (1960-2015). McGowan, a liberal, was not religious and came across as being a bit hostile to Christianity. But he was probably viewed by the predator wing of the Establishment as some right-wing conspiracy theorist nut (in plain language: someone who does his or her own research and questions known liars).

In his book *Weird Scenes Inside the Canyon*, McGowan wrote about Laurel Canyon, California, during the 1960s and early 1970s, where an array of musical artists congregated to create the giant musical hits that provided the soundtrack to those two spectacular eras.

McGowan lists the following American bands and singers, who seemed to come out of nowhere and had the 'red-carpet' rolled out for them and all the 'doors greased and opened': The Byrds, Buffalo Springfield, The Monkees, the Beach Boys, the Mamas and the Papas, The Turtles, The Eagles, Frank Zappa and the Mothers of Invention, Steppenwolf,

Captain Beefheart, CSN, Three Dog Night, Alice Cooper, The Doors; along with such singer/song-writers as Joni Mitchell, Judy Collins, James Taylor, Carole King, Jackson Browne, Judi Sill and David Blue, all of these living together in a small community nestled in the Hollywood Hills.

What seems to be sinister about this jam-packed hippy-type-utopian commune, overlooked by a covert military installation and wandering intelligence personnel, is that nearly all these musicians had military family ties. Also, some of the biggest stars did not make it out alive with such short-lived careers, while their deaths, many aged 27, to this day, are shrouded in mystery.

But, hey, that's all just a big coincidence and we know that the devil, who loves and runs the music industry, hates conspiracy theories. The devil is also instrumental (no pun intended!) in the negative effects of the music genre, especially rock, rap, jazz, R&B, etc.

According to psychologist Dr Laura Sanger, in her research into the music industry: Since the 1930s, sound engineers and physicists, hired by anti-Christian people in 'High Places' (Ephesians 6:12), have been examining how music frequencies can be used to stir-up negative emotional responses in the mass behaviour and hysteria within audiences, causing people to act in certain programmable ways; stripping humans of their humanity by defiling them in the pursuit of the total domination of humanity.

She said: "Part of their strategy is to use sound and music to control humanity. The international tuning of 'A' was changed [in the 1930s, from 435 *Hz] to 440 Hz." She said the Nazi Joseph Goebbels, who ran the radio stations, was involved in this transformation in June 1939. (*Hz, hertz, is a unit of frequency equal to one cycle per second. It is abbreviated Hz and is commonly used to specify the frequency of radio waves.)

"This is a destructive frequency. And what it does is entrains our thoughts towards disharmony, disruption, and disunity. It stimulates our brain into disharmonious resonance," according to Dr Sanger. She added that some Christian musicians are lowering the tone by a few notches to counteract this.

In an article in *Global News* back in 2018, Alan Cross wrote: "There is allegedly something sinister and evil about 440 Hz. It is said that the Rockefeller Foundation had an interest in making sure the

United States adopted the 440 Hz standard in 1935 as part of a 'war on consciousness' leading to 'musical cult control.' Without going too far down this rat hole, this theory says that tuning all music to 440 Hz turns it into a military weapon."

But it is not just tones. There is also the beat of drums worth considering. Rock-and-Roll legend Little Richard has testified that rock music is demonic: "My true belief about Rock 'n' Roll, and there have been a lot of phrases attributed to me over the years, is this: I believe this kind of music is demonic ... a lot of the beats in music today are taken from voodoo, from the voodoo drums. If you study music in rhythms, like I have, you'll see that is true. I believe that kind of music is driving people from Christ. It is contagious." (Little Richard, quoted by Charles White, *The Life and Times of Little Richard*, p. 197). He added: "I was directed and commanded by another power. The power of darkness ... The power that a lot of people don't believe exists. The power of the Devil. Satan."

Mind control is the main method used in voodoo rituals. I'm reminded of Mick Jagger singing "Sympathy for the Devil," and the voodoo drumbeat accompanied by demonic, primitive screams. A song that was sung during a Stones' free concert when a man was stabbed to death in 1969 at Altamont, USA.

There has been some speculation over the years by Western intellectuals writing on culture that major figures in modern music projected their own immorality into the melodies and lyrics of popular songs and tunes. Such works were allegedly inspired by Wagner, Nietzsche, and Arnold Schoenberg (divisor of the unesthetic twelve-tone music), the latter creating twelve-tone music that, in my opinion, is intentionally ambiguous and delayed, and sometimes frustratingly avoiding the resolution of the dissonance, thus the release of emotional tension: Catharsis.

If there was, and still is, a deliberate attempt to subvert the effect of catharsis, then it would appear such an anti-Christian narrative showcasing the absence of a cathartic resolution of emotions could possibly sink below consciousness and influence potentially rebellious-type audiences to embrace secularism and despair.

As Secular Man is driven by endless, unachievable desires; and with no higher destiny, besides music, we can also see such despair in the Absurdist

Godless plays of Samuel Beckett, as well as atheist philosophical literature, music, Surrealist art and cinema: from the Godless Schopenhauer, Wagner, Nietzsche, to Max Ernst and Luis Buñuel.

Finally, the Bible makes it clear about the devil's musical abilities, as Lucifer was a minister of music in Heaven before he got kicked out due to pride and rebellion against God. In Ezekiel 28:13: "…The workmanship of thy [Lucifer] timbrels and of thy pipes was prepared in the that thou was created." Also, Isaiah: 14:11-12: "Thy [Lucifer] pomp is brought down to the grave, and the noise of thy viols [stringed instruments] …"

Chapter 4

That Odd Diversity of Misery and Joy

Isn't it odd that the enormous volume of highly artistic works—from movies, drama, literature, poetry to music—are invariably bleak but give us immense joy? (This is especially evident in the yesteryear world of popular music, but I'll come to that later.)

One wonders, are we better off living in a fallen world after all?—as a perfect one without strife would lack in artistic excellence. But does a world with immense suffering justify moments of optimism through the transient pleasures of the arts, despite their dark themes? After all, one can't have Shakespeare's work without its tragedy, or W.B. Yeats without a terrible beauty being born.

The German philosopher Gottfried Leibniz (1646-1716) believed we live in the best of all possible worlds, despite the pain and injustice that exist. In fact, with the exception of George Berkeley and Leibniz, almost every philosopher from Plato to

Wittgenstein leaned more towards pessimism in their outlook of life. Even in the world of theatre, from the ancient Greeks to contemporary drama, tragedy plays a profound role in defining Western civilization, while evoking sadness and joy resulting in catharsis in audiences. Think about it: besides theatre and cinema, all the TV soap opera dramas infused with misery paradoxically give millions of fans worldwide immense pleasure; similarly, dark, melancholic paintings in the genre of Romanticism ('The Death of Chatterton') are far more stimulating than a Kitsch 'Dogs Playing Poker' by Cassius Coolidge.

But back to the world of popular music, where so much misery has given us so much joy. Such a dichotomy was captured in the 1932 song, "Mad About the Boy," written by the playwright Sir Noel Coward. The song, like most great love songs, is about unrequited love. It is usually sung by female singers, lamenting the odd diversity of misery and joy while being in the metaphorical bondage of such a "foolish" infatuation.

But just because a song is sad or depressing doesn't mean it's without artistic merit, both lyrically and melodically. Any local priest will tell you the many requests they receive for bitter-sweet songs from brides and grooms, who unwittingly want them played for their nuptial ceremony. Songs like "Help Me Make it Through The Night," "Knocking on Heaven's Door," and "You've Lost That Loving Feeling" were popular favourites for those walking up the aisle in recent years.

I once heard of a couple who requested the Tammy Wynette song "D-I-V-O-R-C-E" to be played for their 'first dance' after the wedding ceremony. However, below I've chosen a handful of depressing songs that gave, and still give, great pleasure to music lovers worldwide, despite their depressing lyrics. To narrow the dreariest hits down to the top 5, read on and see if you agree.

Coming in at Number 5 is The Ink Spots, with "We Three (My Echo, My Shadow and Me)." The Ink Spots, who were a vocal group during the 1930s-'40s, made this 1940 song a radio favorite. The song opens with the lyrics of a spiritually tortured, lonesome trio, isolated in the mind of a lost soul searching for love and company:

We three, we're all alone
Living in a memory
My echo, my shadow, and me
We three, we're not a crowd
We're not even company
My echo, my shadow, and me

The song goes on to lament the silvery moonlight that shines up above, and how only 'my echo, my shadow and me' can experience it, 'but where is the one that I love?' The 'three' pledge to wait alone, even till eternity to find the one.

The theme of loneliness is no stranger to existentialist literature. In such a Godless landscape, we are thrown into this world and, ultimately, will die alone. To echo the song's lyrics, Jean-Paul Sartre said: "If you're lonely when you're alone, you're in bad company."

At Number 4, is the 1969 No.1 hit by Zager and Evans, "In the Year 2525." This Brave New World one-hit wonder is not for the technophobe fainthearted. It's the kind of song that could cause a luddite to overdose on Xanax. It opens with the words:

In the year 2525,
If man is still alive,
If woman can survive,
They may find . . .

Subsequent verses multiply the following years and chronicle them as a time when automated machines work our limbs because of an overdependence on technology; pills taken each day to make us think a certain way; marriage becoming obsolete, as babies are conceived "at the bottom of a long glass tube." By the year 9595, Man's reign is through, as humanity has wiped out everything, thus the last verse concludes:

Now it's been 10,000 years
Man has cried a billion tears
For what, he never knew
Now man's reign is through
But through eternal night
The twinkling of starlight
So very far away
Maybe it's only yesterday . . .

Some other hits of 1969, such as the Fifth Dimension's "Aquarius/Let The Sunshine In" or The Archies' "Sugar, Sugar" were far less pessimistic, but they didn't have the impact of '2525'. Works on dystopias are always threatening, as well as robotic technological advancements, which were (and still are) a source of worry to many intellectuals and philosophers.

In the last decades of his life, the existentialist German philosopher Martin Heidegger (1889-1976) spoke about such threats, as opposed to its benefits. Philosophy professor Mark Wrathall wrote: "His preoccupation with 'the technological mode of revealing' was driven by the belief that if we come to experience everything as a mere resource, our ability to lead worthwhile lives will be put at risk. His task as a thinker was to awaken us to the danger of this age, and to point out possible ways for us to avoid the snares of the technological age." The less one hears of this dystopian classic, the sounder one sleeps.

At Number 3, is the song "Eve of Destruction," written by the late P.F. Sloan and sung by Barry McGuire. It was a No.1 hit on Billboard in 1965. Themes in this seminal protest song included the threat of nuclear war, racial tensions, JFK assassination, and bloody middle eastern conflict.

What is most remarkable about this song is that the lyrics were written by a teenage boy. The protagonist of the song is that of a socially conscious person who has been 'Red-pilled,' trying desperately to explain the state of world affairs, which are on a razor's edge. But the Pollyanna respondent keeps replying, "Ah, you don't believe we're on the eve of destruction." Here's a taste of some of the bleak lyrics:

If the button is pushed
There's no running away
There'll be no one to save
With the world in a grave
Take a look around you, boy,
It's bound to scare you, boy
And you tell me over and over and over again my
*   friend*
Ah, you don't believe we're on the eve of destruc-
*   tion*

The song also highlights the hatred in Communism, as well as Selma Alabama, and that marches alone won't solve human rights issues. And it mentions the hypocrisy of some religious who hate their next-door neighbour but "don't forget to say grace."

In Sloan's obituary in the *New York Times* in 2015, Bruce Weber wrote: "The song was controversial; politicians and other musicians debated whether its message, that violence and hypocrisy were a grave threat to civilization, was an accurate depiction of the state of the world, a healthy message to transmit in pop music, or a reasonable representation of the outlook of America's youth. It also changed Mr. Sloan's life."

The eve of spiritual destruction is the theme of my No.2 choice, "Is That All There Is?" In his book *A Secular Age*, the philosopher Charles Taylor wrote that some people long for ultimate meaning, and that longing may end with God. God is always breaking in, stepping through the immanent frame of secularism, according to Taylor. But when 'secular' God makes his appearance, Taylor finds, he sounds just like Peggy Lee singing *Is That All There Is?* The song, arguably the most depressing song ever written, was inspired by the 1896 story 'Disillusionment' (*Enttäuschung*) by Thomas Mann. It sums up precisely the *real* meaning of secularism.

It tells the story of a young girl and the disappointments she experiences throughout her life. Everything seems empty and tinged with the melancholy of all things done. Finally, left with a broken heart when her lover leaves her, her last words confront a way out by suicide. But she finally says she's in no hurry for that ultimate disappointment, uttering in her last breath: "Is that all there is?" (See final chapter, which features this song).

This brings us on to a final, joint fusion of miserable, yet powerful songs: "21st Century Schizoid Man/Epitaph." This song(s) fusion, from the album *The Court of the Crimson King*, by the progressive rock band King Crimson, was released during the height of the Vietnam War in 1969. It was also the era of Woodstock, when Country Joe and the Fish sang the satirical anti-war number, "I-Feel-Like-I'm-Fixin'-to-Die":

And It's one, two three,
What are we fighting for?
Don't ask me, I don't give a damn,
Next stop is Vietnam,
And it's five, six, seven,
Open up the pearly gates,
Well there ain't no time to wonder why,
Whoopee! We're all gonna die

Less satirical but equally serious, the lyrics "21st Century Schizoid Man/Epitaph" depict a series of tragic images and apocalyptic prophecy. The words have on occasions been quoted in his talks by the philosopher Ravi Zacharias, to highlight the ramifications of atheism and relativism. The lyrics begin with neuro-surgeons screaming for more at paranoia's poison door:

Blood rack barbed wire
    Politicians' funeral pyre
    Innocents raped with napalm fire
    Twenty first century schizoid man.
Death seed blind man's greed
    Poets' starving children bleed

> *Nothing he's got he really needs*
> *Twenty first century schizoid man.*

In "Epitaph," the third track in the album, the lyrics point to the wall on which the prophets wrote, which is cracking at the seams, upon the instruments of death, the sunlight brightly gleams when every man is torn apart with nightmares and with dreams, will no one lay the laurel wreath when silence drowns the screams:

> *Confusion will be my epitaph*
> > *As I crawl a cracked and broken path*
> > *If we make it we can all sit back and laugh*
> > *But I fear tomorrow I'll be crying . . .*
> *. . . Knowledge is a deadly friend*
> > *When no one sets the rules*
> > *The fate of all mankind I see*
> > *Is in the hands of fools*
> *Yes I fear tomorrow I'll be crying*

Finally, contrast the lyrics of the above songs with the optimism of Rodgers and Hammer-

stein's "Oh, What a Beautiful Mornin," the opening
song from the hit musical *Oklahoma!*

Oh, what a beautiful mornin'!
Oh, what a beautiful day!
I've got a beautiful feelin'
Ev'rythin's goin' my way.

If only life were so easy.

Chapter 5

Finding it "Easy to be Hard"

Charity Begins at Home, Louis Dalrymple, 1898

The words, "Easy to be Hard," in the title of this chapter refer to the name of a song from the 1968 Broadway rock musical, *Hair*. "Easy to be Hard" was also covered in 1969 by the band, Three Dog Night. The lyrics are quite interesting and psycho-logically highly perceptive:

How can people be so heartless
 How can people be so cruel
 Easy to be hard
 Easy to be cold
How can *people have no feelings*
 How can they ignore their friends
 Easy to be proud
 Easy to say no
Especially *people who care about strangers*
 Care about evil and social injustice

> *Do you only care about the bleeding crowd*
> *How about a needing friend?*

The then-lead singer of Three Dog Night who sang this song is Chuck Negron. He wrote in his autobiography *Three Dog Nightmare* (1999) about his descent into drug abuse and attributes his recovery from heroin addiction to his turning to God in desperation after dropping out from more than 30 drug treatment facilities.

Although the song has theological implications, I want to highlight some other social connotations, expressed aptly in 1 Timothy 5:8: "But if anyone does not provide for his relatives, and especially for members of his household, he has denied the faith and is worse than an unbeliever."

"Easy to be Hard" was written during a time of great unrest in 1960s' America, during the Vietnam war, the Draft, Sexual Revolution, the ethnic disintegration of cities, and disaffected youth. It is about rebellious, anti-war Hippies in New York City, in particular a young woman called Sheila, who is upset that her ideologically driven boyfriend (Berger) seems to care more about 'bleeding crowd' strangers who are in need, as well as *self-interested* social injustices, while Sheila's needs are ignored or secondary.

The last verse of the song is very telling. You probably recognised some of these people at some point in your life. I certainly have met many of them and still do. They are sometimes referred to as social justice warriors (SJWs) or Woke activists. This makes one wonder: Were these people, predominantly anti-Christian, damaged psychologically as a child, deprived of intimate love, and cannot seem to bond to an individual and love him or her before caring about strangers or distant causes? If that is true, bonding more with an ideology or the needs of the 'in-crowd' seem to explain their detachment for those closer to home.

In reaching out to remote causes, they feel proud of themselves by virtue-signalling and championing the 'Other,' as well as being less responsible for the feelings or welfare of an individual friend. For care and loyalty of the individual loved one or friend is to metaphorically 'enter through the narrow gate,' as opposed to the easier-to-enter 'wide gate' favoured by the mass in-crowd (Matthew 7:13-14).

One of the many negative traits associated with these SJWs is they are full of pride with deep-seated convictions. Is it any wonder that the *deep* State sees these useful idiots as model citizens who are easy to control. In WB Yeats's poem, "The Second Coming," he writes: "...The best lack all convictions, while the worst are full of passionate intensity..." The reason for this is because SJWs have replaced God for the *deep* nanny-State, which tells them how to think.

The Christian philosopher JP Moreland once told a story of when he was a young student and had "a thing" for a girl at college but she was more interested in fighting for some other "bigger" cause; probably an anti-war movement during the Vietnam conflict in the mid-1960s. Intimacy with fellow-student Mr Moreland or embracing God was not for her. This is because the SJW craves moral reputation from the herd and a craving to be popular.

The Bible says: "Be careful not to display your righteousness merely to be seen by people. Otherwise, you have no reward with your Father in Heaven. Thus whenever you do charitable giving, do not blow a trumpet before you, as the hypocrites do in synagogues and on streets so that people will praise them." (Matthew 6:1-2)

In the past in literature, we see other, similar-type SJW characters, as in Dickens's "Bleak House," where Mrs Jellyby, an English "telescopic philanthropist," is more concerned and obsessed with an obscure African tribe but having no regard for charity beginning with her own husband and family who struggle to survive, while her house lies in ruins.

In fact, the current hijacked West has metaphorically become "Bleak House," with 'Mrs Jellyby' political leaders, who seem to treat their own indigenous citizens with contempt and are more focused on representing other causes in foreign lands, even at the expense of their own people. This self-centred "philanthropic" insanity is certainly not done through love or kindness.

In 2016, *Philanthropy Daily* journalist Jacqueline Pfeffer Merrill, wrote: "Dickens' critique of telescopic philanthropy is likewise germane today, when Americans give $15 billion [*See latest figure below] annually to global causes. Of course, many of these causes are very worthy, but we must be thoughtful about balancing global causes and urgent needs in our own neighbourhoods and country, and about whether we understand the needs of far-away people well enough to do good. So far, Dickens' time and ours were alike." [*Since the war began, the Biden administration and the U.S. Congress have directed more than $75 billion, and still counting early-2024, in assistance to Ukraine. Meanwhile, Maui is reduced to ashes, while its citizens are crying out for aid].

Pfeffer Merrill is right about many causes being worthy, but the key issue is prioritising concerns closer to one's own 'home.' Consider 'telescope philanthropy' in Ireland: Integration Green Party coalition Minister, Roderic O'Gorman, announced Ireland's soft-touch asylum policy online in eight different languages. The tweets were posted in February of 2021, and they outlined the government's plan to end Direct Provision and provide "own-door" accommodation to any and all asylum seekers in Ireland after just a few months. They were posted in English, Irish, Arabic, Georgian, Albanian, Somalian, Urdu, and French. Meanwhile, thousands of indigenous Irish homeless people live on the streets in tents, and over 100,000 Irish children and young people are on hospital waiting lists, according to the National Treatment Purchase Fund. Such telescopic philanthropy inviting the Third World to come and be housed in Ireland for free would make even Mrs Jellyby blush.

This is what happens when one rebels against the Logos. In his short story, "Things That Fly," Douglas Coupland seems to have a remedy: "… I need God to help me love, as I seem beyond being able to love."

But most SJWs hate the God of Christianity. A couple of years ago, Black Lives Matter activists cornered a woman at a restaurant in Washington DC because she wouldn't raise her fist in solidarity with their chants that "white silence is violence." One of the protesters in front accusingly asks, "Are you a Christian?"

Finally, charity should begin at home (if the members of that home are not deviant idiots), avoid SJWs, who obviously need God to help them love intimately, as they reach out to save and help strangers or perpetuate doomed, woke causes in far-away lands. Many of them might end their days alone or super-glued to a painting at the local art gallery, or disrupting a sporting event by streaking around a football pitch with "Just Stop Oil" tattooed to the cheeks of their rear end. Love them, be kind to them, but to repeat, avoid the Greenpeace warriors, as they arrive wearing face masks and lay candles and teddy bears on the sand when a dead Orca is washed ashore with a face-mask stuck in his blowhole. SJWs should instead spare a thought for the unfairly demonised, Caucasian heterosexual males—not the killer whales.

Chapter 6

Music Inspired by
Throwaway Remarks, Nature, and God

Have you ever wondered what inspired some of the world's most popular lyrics and melodies? Consider Garth Brooks' country and western monster hit "Friends in Low Places," arguably the most popular singalong ditty over the past 30 years.

From a theological perspective, the song's chorus highlights the camaraderie in a community of sinners, where the protagonist finds solace in the company of his friends, whose lives of hardship in a fallen world are similar to his life. I don't particularly like the song, but I'm intrigued by the origin of its lyrics.

According to Earl Bud Lee, one of the song's co-writers, the idea of the hit came about when he and some friends had eaten lunch in an eatery in Nashville. After the meal, Lee discovered that he had forgotten his money, hence he couldn't pay the cheque. When asked how he was going to pay the bill, he allegedly said, "Don't worry. I have friends in low places: I know the cook."

When Lee's song-writing buddy, Dewayne Blackwell, heard this, he felt as if the line had potential for a song. Some months later at a party, the pair, writing on paper napkins, began writing what was to become a massive hit. They later approached Brooks, a then-struggling musician, and the rest is Country & Western history.

Another throwaway remark that inspired a classic of a more sophisticated song is the 1967 hit, "A Whiter Shade of Pale," sung by British group, Procol Harum. I regard this as one of the greatest songs of all time, but I haven't got a clue what it's about (I hope it's not blasphemous!). However, its origin is less poetic and more psychedelic.

The inspiration for the song's idea is explained by the band's lyricist, Keith Reid. He said he got the title and starting structure of the song at a party, when he overheard someone saying to a woman: "You've turned a whiter shade of pale." Reid and band members Gary Brooker and Matthew Fisher completed writing/composing the song, with its Bach-derived instrumental melody. The result, when released, was it reached Number One in the UK charts for eight weeks and selling over 10 million copies worldwide.

It is not quite clear what is going on in this seemingly, emotionally sentimental song but, like all similar songs, the pathos has echoes of a fallen world. The Beatle John Lennon said it was his favourite song and would play it regularly on his jukebox.

In another throwaway remark on the origin of a song, the great soul singer Dionne Warwick had her first solo recording of the song "Don't Make Me Over" in 1962. However, during a tiff about wanting to sing another song, Warwick yelled at composer Burt Bacharach, "Don't make me over, man!" and stormed out of his office. Bacharach and lyricist Hal David quickly composed a song inspired by what she said and offered it to her. It was also covered in 1966 by the British Merseybeat band, The Swinging Blue Jeans. The song's lyrics has the protagonist say, "just love me for all my faults." Jesus said, "love your enemies and pray for those who persecute you" (Matthew 5:43-48).

Another love song was composed by James Thornton, when in 1898 he wrote "When You Were Sweet Sixteen." He was inspired by his own words when his wife, Bonnie, asked him if he still loved her. Thornton replied, "I love you like I did when you were sweet sixteen," hence, the song was over the past 100 years covered by the world's greatest singers and sold millions of copies. One of the core messages in the Bible is love and the greatest hits of all time echo this message.

Even God's great creation of the solar system inspires popular music, with such orchestral suites as "The Planets," by Gustav Holst, despite ignoring some astrological factors. From the cosmos and philosophy to theology: When it comes to artistic inspiration, it's hard to beat the Bible. The 1960s' Number One hit song "Turn! Turn! Turn!" was written (arranged) in the late-1950s by the late Pete Seeger. The lyrics, except for the title, are taken almost verbatim from the *Book of Ecclesiastes*.

Another example of Bible verse set to popular music is Boney M's "Rivers of Babylon" (Psalm 137:1), which stayed at Number One in the UK charts for five weeks in 1978. In fact, the Psalms are infused with references to singing the praises of Our Lord.

But it's not just the words from God or humans that inspire such great music. We also see this mimesis when music imitates nature and the creatures created by God. It can reasonably be assumed that Nikolai Rimsky-Korsakov's orchestral interlude "Flight of the Bumblebee" was inspired by the chaotic sound caused by honey-making creatures as they ascend from the hive.

Even creatures from the ocean can inspire. Many years ago, the late Irish Taoiseach (PM), Charles Haughey, said he believed the original source of music that inspired an ancient Irish folk song was the sound of a humpbacked whale. He tells the story of three men at sea, sitting in their *currach, motionless, and that the hull of the boat would act as a reverberating sounding board for the 'music' of a whale, which passes by the Blasket Islands, off County Kerry's Dingle west-coast. (*This is a type of Irish boat with a wooden frame, over which animal skins or hides were stretched.)

Haughey, who bought Inishvickillane, the most southerly of the Blasket Islands, theorized: "A yachtsman friend from Cork, Eugene O'Malley, was anchored one night at the inish [one of the islands], and he suddenly heard this [whale] 'music' and was intrigued by it … He later made a recording of it ["Port na bPúcaí" (Port of Pucks)] and sent it to National Geographic, which in turn sent it back to him with a tape recording of the humpbacked whale. O'Malley then put the two recordings side by side and they sounded almost identical."

Also at sea, the mimeses of another tune that was probably inspired by fowl of the sky, is "The Lonesome Boatman," composed by Irish folk-music duo, Finbar and Eddie Fury. It features the haunting sound of a tin-whistle sounding like the squawk of a seagull echoing high above a boatman as he casts his nets. Similarly, but less squawky, is Fleetwood Mac's 1968 Number One classic, "Albatross."

The composition and arrangement of this beautiful masterpiece conjure up a calm sea setting beside a remote beach, with cymbals imitating the sound of waves gently flowing across the sand, accompanied by the dreamlike solo from Peter Green's incredible guitar riff. The song, which was written by Green (the founder of Fleetwood Mac), was inspired by the 1798 poem "The Rime of the Ancient Mariner" by English poet Samuel Taylor Coleridge. Themes with water are rife in theology.

From being inspired by throwaway remarks to mimeses in nature, to the words of Plato: "Music is a moral law. It gives a soul to the universe, wings to the mind, flight to the imagination, a charm to sadness, gaiety, and life to everything. It is the essence of order, and leads to all that is good and just and beautiful."

While I partially agree with Plato's sentiments, the ancient Greeks never quite got their theology in order to merge with the Logos (God). Plato was probably attributing such music with Apollo, the daughters of Zeus, or the concept of Platonic forms. For it is not music that is the moral law, essence of order, and all things beautiful. It is God: The Logos incarnate.

At Christmas time, as you stroll through the shopping malls of suburbia and the metropolis main streets, you'll no doubt hear the secular, saccharine, elevator musak of "White Christmas" or "Winter Wonderland"—compared to the Divine music of "O Holy Night," sung by charity fundraising carol singers outside the malls' doors and on the sidewalks. I know which bucket I'll be inspired to chuck my spare change into.

Chapter 7

Strange Songs

Before discussing songs with strange, mysterious lyrics, it is worth first mentioning the early years and key eras when such songs were in the music charts: The 1960s to the end of the 1970s.

Many cultural observers of the music industry throughout these eras often comment on the dark side of popular music and speculate on possible psyops elements to create unrest and chaos amongst the Boomer generations and beyond.

Is it a coincidence that the when the Boomers reached adulthood in the mid-1960s, they looked like they were well-socially engineered to be good little model citizens and obey the State, despite causing some civil unrest that was unwittingly advantageous to the State—and often looked like it was caused by the State. The classical Hegelian Dialectic: Thesis, antithesis, synthesis (problem, reaction, solution).

If the Boomer "scruffy/lazy" hippies thought they were rebellious and against 'The Man' during Woodstock in 1969, they were greatly mistaken. Instead, they unwittingly played into the hands of 'The Man' by being stoned en masse, while collectively screwing their way to Hell, unaware of the misdirection propaganda from a controlled mainstream media (compared to today, it was a ministry of half-truths).

Yes, the 1960s was a key epoch for ushering in massive social upheaval, mass hysteria (Beatlemania, etc.) and herd behaviour against the once-traditional, Western culture of Christendom. An anti-culture which has culminated today where tampon dispensers are installed in the men's toilets of the Irish House of Parliament (the Dail).

The situation in Canada is worse. According to the New York Post: "Tampons and sanitary napkins are now available in men's bathrooms at the Canadian Parliament under a new policy from Prime Minister Justin Trudeau that requires all federally regulated employers—including airports and military bases—to offer free menstrual products in all washrooms, regardless of gender noted on the door."

But back to 1965: The year the 'Church of Nice,' the Second Vatican Council concluded. It was also the date when the Number One hit song that heralded in the year was Barry McGuire's aptly titled "Eve of Destruction," written by PF Sloan; a year that saw the birth of the Sexual Revolution, two years before the 'Summer of Love' [recreational sex, drugs and rock'n'roll].

However, one such observer who sceptically reflected on the music industry of the Sixties and Seventies was the writer of conspiracy theory books (many would say 'spoiler alert' books), David McGowan (R.I.P.). McGowan, a liberal, was not religious and came across as being a bit hostile to Christianity. But he was probably viewed by the predator wing of the Establishment as some right-wing fundamentalist conspiracy theorist nut (in plain language: someone who does his own research and questions known liars, and is later, in most cases, proven right in his theories).

In his book *Weird Scenes Inside the Canyon*, McGowan wrote about Laurel Canyon (California) in the 1960s and early 1970s, where an array of musical artists congregated to create the giant musical hits that provided the soundtrack to those two spectacular eras.

McGowan lists the following American bands and singers, who seemed to come out of nowhere and had the 'red-carpet' rolled out for them and all the 'doors greased and opened': Bands and singers like The Byrds, Buffalo Springfield, The Monkees, the Beach Boys, the Mamas and the Papas, The Turtles, The Eagles, Frank Zappa and the Mothers of Invention, Steppenwolf, Captain Beefheart, CSN, Three Dog Night, Alice Cooper, The Doors; along with such singer/songwriters as Joni Mitchell, Judy Collins, James Taylor, Carole King, Jackson Browne, Judi Sill and David Blue, all living together in a small community nestled in the Hollywood Hills.

What seems to be sinister about this jam-packed Hippy-type-utopic commune, overlooked by a covert military installation and wandering intelligence personnel, is that nearly all these musicians had military family ties. Also, many did not make it out alive with such short-lived careers, while their deaths, many aged 27, to this day, are shrouded in mystery.

But, hey, that's all just a big coincidence and we know that the devil, who loves and runs the music industry, hates conspiracy theories. The devil is also instrumental (no pun intended!) in the negative effects of the music genre, especially rock, rap, jazz, etc.

According to psychologist Dr Laura Sanger, in her research into the music industry: since the 1930s, sound engineers and physicists, hired by anti-Christian people in 'High Places' (Ephesians 6:12), have been examining how music frequencies can be used to stir-up negative emotional responses in the mass behaviour and hysteria within audiences, causing people to act in certain programmable ways; stripping humans of their humanity by defiling them in pursuit of the total domination of humanity.

She said: "Part of their strategy is to use sound and music to control humanity. The international tuning of 'A' was changed [in the 1930s, from 435 Hz] to 440 Hz." She said the Nazi Joseph Goebbels was involved in this transformation in June 1939. "This is a destructive frequency. And what it does is entrains our thoughts towards disharmony, disruption, and disunity. It stimulates our brain into disharmonious resonance," according to Dr Sanger. But it is not just the melody that can affect us psychology and spiritually. Lyrics also play a powerful role. Conscious and/or subliminal messages can affect us positively and/or negatively. Consider these strange lyrics below, which may, or may not, be psy-ops driven.

"Horse With No Name," 1971. Band: America.

There were many other musicians whose songs contain strange lyrics, possibly unrelated to any psy-ops theory. One such British-American group during the early-1970s, which all had US military family ties, was America [I mention the military ties in relation to David McGowans theories]. Their one-hit wonder in 1971 was called "A Horse with No Name."

Ostensibly, the lyrics to this song indicate it is a story about a person riding across the desert on a horse. The nomadic odyssey has vague echoes of ancient desert scenes with lone prophets, inspired by the words of the Holy Spirit, warning about immoral behaviour and future events. Along the way, the singer, sounding very much like Neill Young, sings about the various scenes he sees. As for the horse with no name: Music critics have speculated that 'horse' is the slang term for heroin, and that the animal in the song is a metaphor for that drug and the hallucinations it causes: The psychedelic desert scenes.

Writing in *Interesting Literature,* Dr Oliver Tearle from Loughborough University says: "Is 'horse' meant as slang for heroin in the song? Originally titled 'Desert Song', 'A Horse with No Name' had its origins in the miserable rain. Dewey Bunnell of the band later explained that he 'wanted to capture the imagery of the desert, because I was sitting in this room in England, and it was rainy. The rain was starting to get to us, and I wanted to capture the desert and the heat and the dryness.'."

The song begins with the singer describing the desert landscape, with its plants, birds, rocks, sand, hills, "things," and a buzzing fly. The singer, although his skin begins to turn red from exposure from the sun, seems happy to be in the dry wilderness, as the solitude escapes him from other humans who can do you wrong; and, because of the solitude, he can 'lose' his identity and the psychological torments of the Id. Jesus said: 'Whoever finds his life will lose it, and whoever loses his life for my sake will find it' (Matthew: 10:39).

As for the nameless horse: The singer lets it go free as the desert looked like it was turning to sea (a mirage due to the scorching sun?). Many years ago, I attended a concert by America, and they left 'Horse with no Name' as the last song, to the rapturous applause of the packed concert hall.

Co-founder member of the band, Dan Peek, was a pioneer in contemporary Christian music. After he left the band in 1977, he released a second solo album, 1984's *Doer of the Word*, which hit number 2 in the Christian charts. In a remake of the song "Lonely People", he changed some of the song's lyrics to reflect his Christian faith, with the lines, "And ride that highway in the sky" and "You never know until you try" became "And give your heart to Jesus Christ". Peek died in his sleep of uremic pericarditis on July 24, 2011, at the age of 60 at his home in Farmington, Missouri.

"Everyone's Gone to the Moon," 1965, written/composed and sung by Johnathan King (Not to be confused with a Christian PhD scholar of the same name)

If ever a song was strange and mysterious, then Jonathan King's 1965 hit record must fit the bill. Like the song "A Whiter Shade of Pale," King's lyrics are haunting and baffling, but the melody touches the soul. And as it is unlikely that everyone could go to the moon, one wonders what the metaphor means.

It has been suggested that The Moon was the name of a pub in Cambridge, close to the university where King studied as a young student. If there *was* such a pub, then one can easily imagine some student saying, "They've all gone to The Moon." If not a pub, could it mean everyone has gone crazy (loony moon-bats)? There is also a suggestion that the lyrics were a satire of the "Dylan school." Although the song didn't reach top of the charts, it sold four-million copies worldwide. In one verse, the lyrics read: "…Church full of singing, out of tune…".

One wonders, during that time, as well as today, how many churches were/are not 'singing from the same hymn sheet.' King was, during his pop-music career, no saint, and he certainly was no friend of Christianly during his musical years. In fact, he was involved in a sex scandal an imprisoned. But regardless of King the man, one cannot disregard his classic song.

Here is a sample of two verses:

...Eyes full of sorrow
Never wet
Hands full of money
All in debt
Sun coming out in
The middle of June
Everyone's gone to the moon

...Cars full of motors
Painted green
Mouths full of chocolate
Covered cream
Arms that can only
Lift a spoon, everyone's gone to the moon

I do not believe that King was a prophet back then, but in 1965, green cars (EVs) generally did not exist on the roads. But today, there are lots of them worldwide. One can imagine seeing a rich kid in an EV licking an ice-cream, while in the mines in Congo/Africa, child-labour is used in numerous mines to get lithium to run the EV batteries. Children mining to retrieve this probably can hardly 'lift a spoon' after a long day's work.

Also, the song came out shortly after the first-ever broadcasts of starving children in Africa on TV, which went mainstream into nearly all European households in 1965. Catholic churches and schools regularly handed out 'poor boxes for the African babies,' and many Catholic charities were set up to send overseas aid to the famine-stricken areas.

In the above lyrics, King's meaning hypothetically seem to juxtapose the rich West, with kids eating their ice creams, compared to famine-stricken sub-Saharan Africa, where the starving children can hardly lift a spoon. The Irish singer/songwriter, Gilbert O'Sullivan, had a 1971 hit with the song "Nothing Rhymed;" a song that reflected the 'arms that can only lift a spoon' lyrics. Below is a sample verse, arguably the most profound lyrics in the history of popular music:

When I'm drinking my Bonaparte Shandy
Eating more than enough apple pies
Will I glance at my screen
And see real human beings
Starve to death right in front of my eyes

"Mister Turnkey", 1969, Zager and Evans:

This song is the B-side of arguably the most depressing song of all time, "In the Year 2525." "Mister Turnkey" is about a man who murders a woman and feels great remorse for taking her life. In prison, he pleads with his jailer, saying he needed a woman, but women were not interested in him. However:

> *...But Mister Turnkey, she looked at me with flirtin' eyes*
> *Mister Turnkey, she was lovelier than oil lights*
> *Mister Turnkey, she led me on, she led me on*
> *She know she wasn't going to let me love her*
>
> *Mister Turnkey, I forced that girl in Wichita Falls*
> *Mister Turnkey, I'm sittin' here cryin' in coveralls*
> *Mister Turnkey, don't want to be the man I am...*
> *Mister Turnkey, I've nailed my left wrist to your wall...*

There are echoes of a plea for redemption in the final lyrics of this song. Shame and guilt also feature heavily. Without God, there is no shame or guilt. The lion that forcibly copulates with a lioness does not rape her. Animals are not moral agents, but we are.

Haitian Divorce, Steely Dan, 1976

When I first listened to this great song in the mid-'70s, it was the weirdest track I had ever heard. I could not make out what the strange instrument was playing on the record ('talkbox'), not to mention the uncoded, meaning of the darkish lyrics.

The song is by the American band duo, Steely Dan, written by Donald Fagen and Walter Becker. It was included in their album, "The Royal Scam."

Set in Haiti, an alleged cursed country with a tumultuous past, conjuring up images of voodoo, zombies, earthquakes, and a rumoured political pact with the devil, the lyrics in the story have some interesting theological themes.

A country where Evangelical Protestantism represents a third of the country's population of over nine million people, increasing numbers of Haitians, both at home and abroad, practice various forms of Protestant Christianity.

As for the crux of the story from a Catholic perspective: What could be more theologically Catholic than divorce, not to mention the sin of promiscuity, and having a child out of wedlock?

The lyrics tell the bizarre yarn of a couple called Charlie and Marlene, who travel to Haiti to get a quick divorce, as such 'quickies' were available in the country during the 1970s. From a Christian perspective, the song highlights a Godless pair of liberals who confuse sexual/socio liberation with, in reality, being a slave to one's own lustful passions by doing 'what thou wilt.' Despite if this is the song's message (some of Steely Dan's songs can be quite satirical), it is one of my all-time guilty pleasures. The music arrangement, melody, beat, and lyrics are highly impressive.

Donald Fagen, in a 1976 interview with *Sounds*, said of the story behind the song: "It's a fierce and terrible ritual. I'll tell you that. You wouldn't want your sister to have a Haitian divorce, believe me. It was the quick divorce, without too much red tape. If you can say 'incompatibility of character' in French you're as good as gold. But we added a few elements to the ceremony itself."

The song tells the story about a woman who goes to Haiti for her divorce. While she is there, she has recreational sex with a man, climaxing in cinematic terms in the lines:

Now we dolly back
Now we fade to black

The woman, after having some 'fun' and 'drinking zombie from the coco shell (rum-base cocktail), returns to America, and discovers she is pregnant: "Some babies grow in a peculiar way."

Steely Dan's lyrics are vague and mysterious and their melodies jazzy. In some of their songs, the themes are sleazy, telling short stories with literary, TV, and cinematic references, infused with slang, about people who are slaves to their destructive passions. Fallen sinners in a Fallen World. In a nutshell: Theology on steroids.

"Nights in White Satin," Moody Blues, 1967.

The enigmatic classic song, "Nights in White Satin" from the album *Days of Future Past,* has sold millions worldwide. It has also appeared on film soundtracks as well as inspiring more than 60 cover versions, thanks to Justin Hayward's haunting lyrics and melody.

The hopeless romantic male protagonist in the song is caught between the odd diversity of misery and joy, reflecting maudlinly the end of one love affair while embarking on another. But it's not the singing in the song that I want to theologically focus on, it's the spoken-poem at the end of the track that intrigues me. It's called "Late Lament," and it is written and narrated by the band's drummer, Graeme Edge.

The first verse goes like this:

Breathe deep the gathering gloom
Watch lights fade from every room
Bedsitter people look back and lament
Another day's useless energy is spent
Impassioned lovers wrestle as one;
Lonely man cries for love and has none;
New mother picks up and suckles her son;
Senior citizens wish they were young

Theologically, this verse evokes the fallen world in which we live. Melancholic situations in which ordinary people find themselves trapped, some sad, some pleasant. Lamentations of regret, emptiness, loneliness, remorse, intense passion, the passing of time, permeate the poem.

It continues:

> *Cold-hearted orb that rules the night*
> *Removes the colours from our sight*
> *Red is grey is yellow white*
> *But we decide which is right*
> *And which is an illusion*

Theologically, despite being a great poem, the final verse is a post-modern narrative of Modern Man. The narrator suggests perception is reality, thus, we can create our own reality. There are also echoes of solipsism, perhaps unwittingly, in the narrative. But it is nonetheless quite clever, in that 'appearance and reality' is a major philosophical problem. Think about it: At night under the orb of moonlight, every external thing red looks grey, and yellow white. Regarding language, on Christianity there are no grey areas. Jesus said: "But let your 'Yes' be 'Yes,' and your 'No,' 'No.' For whatever is more than these is from the evil one" (Matthew 5:57).

Chapter 8

The Psychological Power
of Melody and Lyrics

Our auditory perception is our main portal to communications with other humans, in song lyrics and melodies, and the vibe-tones of the natural world, from the sounds of the forest, ocean and other weather phenomena.

The acoustic world has the power to evoke deep emotions and pathos that touch the depths of our souls and influence our behavior. Sometimes, this happens subliminally. In the opening melody of Elvis Presley's "Kentucky Rain" (1970), we hear an instrument sounding like rain falling (or teardrops) on a rooftop. The rainfall adds pathetic fallacy to the narrative.

The song is about a man driving through rural Kentucky, in the pouring rain, in search for a woman he loves who fled from him. Similarly, the 1972 song sung by Harry Neilson, "Without You," is about heartbreak, and the musical instrument in the opening melody vaguely sounds like teardrops slowly falling.

Here, the acoustic world mirrors our emotional state. "Without You," from a Christian perspective, is also an idolatrous song, where the heartbroken protagonist worships a woman who left him and vaguely implies 'ending it all' as he can't live or *give* without her. This lost, infatuated, fictional chap should have read the opening lines of Amazing Grace:

Amazing grace, how sweet the sound
That saved a wretch like me
I once was lost, but now I am found
Was blind, but now I see.

Listening to music, our eardrums seem to 'dance' to the sound waves in such an acoustic environment where the auditory system picks up oscillations in the acoustic spectrum. Never underestimate the psychological power of lyrics and melody.

The song "You'll Never Walk Alone" (1945) has echoes of, and seems to be inspired by, Psalm 23, one of the greatest Psalms in the Bible. This song is Liverpool FC's anthem and soccer fans sing it passionately en masse in the stadium with the fervour of a religious ceremony. In 1963, a single of the song became a massive hit, sung by the local Liverpool group, Gerry and the Pacemakers.

Writing in *Thrive Global* in 2022, regarding an adaptation from his best-selling book *Amplified*, author Frank Fitzpatrick said: "One of the most powerful ways to influence emotions and consciousness is to set words to memorable music. Add engaging images to this mix and you have what holders of ancient wisdom have known for thousands of years as the ultimate power over the populace."

Fitzpatrick goes on to say that adding music (melody and accompaniment) to a lyrical statement or message activates more areas of the human brain than words alone and can make that message "stickier"—triggering our emotions and memory.

The American writer Nathaniel Hawthorne (1804-1864) said: "Words—so innocent and powerless as they are, as standing in a dictionary, how potent for good and evil they become in the hands of one who knows how to combine them."

This is especially true in the case of metaphors. Is the 'You' in Lou Reed's song "Perfect Day" a met-

aphor for heroin? Although Reed denies this inter-
pretation, many have speculated that it is. The song
is included in the soundtrack for *Trainspotting*, a
film about the lives of heroin addicts. Do the lyrics
"I thought I was someone else" hypothetically sug-
gest an altered state of mind? Or, "You keep me
hanging on" mean waiting for that next fix?

And what about the song "White Christmas."
Does this popular 'classic' de-Christ that holy day,
where *"let it snow, let it snow, let it snow"* is what the
true meaning of the day is all about? Think about it:
The day celebrated by Christians for the birth of
Christ also becomes a time for "Chestnuts Roasting
on an Open Fire" and "Rudolph the Red-Nosed
Reindeer." These songs, with excellent melodies and
great lyrics, and many more like them, either wit-
tingly or unwittingly parody that sacred day, as they
are played all across the West in the shopping malls
during that peak-consumer season of *'let us spend,
let us spend, let us spend'*.

Despite being un-Christian, these songs are classics and seduce the listener, as the 'best' tunes are
played in Hell. Which brings me to the classic,
"Sympathy for the Devil" by the Rolling Stones. As
mentioned in Chapter 3, mind control is the main

method used in voodoo rituals. I'm reminded of Mick Jagger singing "Sympathy for the Devil," and the voodoo drum-beat accompanied by demonic, primitive screams. A song that was sung during a Stones' free concert when a man was stabbed to death in 1969 at Altamont, USA.

Not only are the lyrics of this song seductive, but the beat is contagious, luring many a young person to get up and dance, rave-like, to the sounds of Hell. There is something primordial about the song, as if we are epigenetically programmed to dance to its jungle-beat tones.

Fitzpatrick, again: "Some people listen closely to lyrics, even singing along with them, while others have little idea or care for what is being said in the words of their favorite songs. A song with a great beat, that we love to play to get us pumped up at the gym, may have expressions of profanity, prejudice or more subtle negative messages that defy the mood and state of consciousness we are seeking to obtain, not to mention our own beliefs and value systems."

Expressions of profanity and subtle negative messages certainly feature in some of the West's greatest songs. One good example is the John Lennon monster world-wide hit in 1971, "Imagine"—a New World Order anthem if ever there was one. Despite its popularity, I never liked "Imagine," regarding its lyrics and melody. I find the lyrics maudlin and the melody naval-gazing. It's also paradoxical, in that it asks to imagine "no religion," while unwittingly replacing it with a secular religion: The ideology of a New World Order.

In spring 2024, writing in *Anthropoetics: The Journal of Generative Anthropology*, Matthew Taylor said: "[...] In almost every line, 'Imagine' expresses itself as religion, puts forward religious propositions, and assume a religious structure. Ironically, the religious elements woven so skilfully (if unintendedly) into 'Imagine' may explain why it continues to grip so many and never goes out of style."

Another song that grips many and has stood the test of time, is REM's "Losing My Religion" (1991). Beginning with the infectious mandolin riff, a discerning listener might wonder is the protagonist of the song singing about religion or a relationship.

In a *New York Times* interview from 1991, singer/songwriter Michael Stipe said the song was about "romantic expression," and noted that the phrase "losing my religion" was actually a Southern US expression referring to being at the end of one's rope.

In classical music, many audiences probably felt at the end of their rope when they heard Wagner's "Tristan und Isold" back in 1865. Where songs like "Losing My Religion" have beginning, middle, and end, Wagner's controversial piece could be described as nihilistic, in that it seems like a deliberate attempt to subvert the effect of cathartic resolution of emotions, similar to the plays of Theatre of the Absurd, and its absence of logical narrative and denouement.

Mark Twain, on a visit to Germany, heard *Tristan* at Bayreuth. He said: "I know of some, and have heard of many, who could not sleep after it, but cried the night away..." In the 1865 edition of the *Allgemeine musikalische Zeitung,* it reported: "Not to mince words, it is the glorification of sensual pleasure, tricked out with every titillating device, it is unremitting materialism, according to which human beings have no higher destiny than, after living the life of turtle doves, 'to vanish in sweet odours, like a breath'."

Chapter 9

The Spectre of a Smirking Demon

When I see what passes for high culture today or stroll through city streets that resemble a giant car park for tall spaceships, surrounded by tents for the homeless, I wonder is the West possessed by a grotesque, smirking demon. And when I think back to the past, despite all its flaws, I lament and feel like sparing a thought for today's luddites, with whom I identify when it comes to aesthetics and beauty.

Beyond Eden and after The Fall, there has never been a golden epoch. But let's briefly look at a couple of comparisons, mostly music-wise, and the relative positives and negatives of two separate eras. Where to begin? Musically, we never had it so bad at the beginning and beyond the second decade of the 21st Century.

Aside from dreadful 'music,' with the demise of the vinyl LP and 45-record, we've gone from analogue to digital to anomie. Let me first explain the 'anomie' reference, a phrase coined by French sociologist Emile Durkheim, near the end of the 19th Century.

One aspect of anomie is soulless alienation. We see good examples of this in the gigantic, Brutalist shopping malls of suburbia, covered in glass and gigantic slabs of stone, and inhabited by zombie-like creatures dressed in yoga pants and tracksuits, wearing headphones while staring into their iPhones as they waddle like penguins hunting for the best bargains. They can't even hear the dreadful mall muzak that pollutes the air in these gigantic, Godless hellholes.

Compared to the consumerism of yesteryear, where one strolled through a village or High Street in search of goods or went to the cinema, Durkheim's version of anomie has gone from a relatively unpleasant experience to the pits of Hell, despite the techno clones thinking they have the world in their hands.

It's true the future of cinema lies in handhelds, but nothing compares to the big screen. During the 1970s, my experience of wild sex was kissing in the back row of the movies on a Saturday night. What relatively innocent times compared to today.

Now, we live in an age where producers and directors are tailoring their movies to online viewers, not to mention the abundance of online pornography. According to statistics, young people are opting for online viewing instead of the 'box-office' experience of yore.

Independent movie theatres, even multiplex-cinemas, are a thing of the past. The average young person watches a movie or listens to music on a personal device, all alone by himself.

Consider the purchase of music today and in the past: Let's call the following hypothetical character, 23-year-old 'Traditional Bob,' born in 1944. Prior to the satanic turbo-hijacking of the West, 'Bob' graduated from high school and served his apprenticeship as an electrician. A lover of the Arts, he has read almost all the classics and loves the theatre.

One Saturday afternoon, he left his house and got onto a bus to visit the nearest music store, which has long-since been converted to a money-laundering racket, operating ostensibly as an iPhone store. On the bus, 'Bob' sits upstairs and has a smoke, while chatting to a stranger who obliged 'Bob' for a 'light' for his cigarette.

Getting off the bus, 'Bob' enters the music store and browses around it before buying the latest Number 1 record or popular LP. 'Bob' recently broke up with his girlfriend, but he meets a young lady in the store, whom he's met on several earlier occasions while browsing. She has the same musical interests as 'Bob,' and he asks her out on a date, to which she agrees.

The hipster behind the counter chats to 'Bob,' telling him about the latest band to watch out for and recommending an upcoming concert. On his way home, Bob decides to drop into a little chapel, which years later has now been converted to an adult store/'massage' parlour with a flashing neon sign of a dildo over the front door. Bob says a prayer then continues on his way home. When he arrives home, after chatting to another stranger on the bus, he sits down sipping a cup of tea from a beautifully painted Japanese teacup while marvelling at the artwork on the LP album cover.

He then places the LP on the record player, puts the needle on the vinyl, sits back and listens to the tracks. Some of his friends visit 'Bob' later that day for coffee, and they'll all listen to the LP and talk about it to one another, praising and/or criticising some tracks.

The quality of the tracks on vinyl is far superior to digital, as digital requires storage space, thus, the music (audio) gets compressed, losing some of its details but 'gaining' practicality regarding mobility and efficiency. With vinyl, we get the original recordings ('masters') of the album/record. To draw an analogy, it's like comparing watching a singer perform in a concert or viewing the film of it on your iPhone.

Nowadays, the older senior-citizen 'Bob' brings his grandchildren on walks to the park to feed the ducks in the pond. His wife, the lady he met many years ago in the music store, stays at home baking cookies and preparing a tea party for her adult children and grandchildren. She tells 'Bob', not to smoke a cigarette in the presence of the kids.

Now, consider the 'convenience' and 'efficiency' that today brings us, at the push of a button or the click of a 'mouse': Meet 'Zoomer Jack,' a 24-year-old born in the year 2000. 'Jack,' who has been single all his life, is an atheist and alleged vegan, who eats the odd beef burger (why are so many vegans and plutocratic governments against eating meat and hetero-marriage? Bible answer: "Now the Spirit speaketh expressly that in the later times some shall depart from the faith giving heed to seducing spirits and doctrines of devils... Forbidding to marry, *and commanding* to abstain from meats, which God hath created to be received with thanksgiving of them which believe and know the truth." [Timothy: Chapter 4].)

'Jack,' who worships the State but hates the Bible, which he never read, graduated with a BA in Gender Studies. For the past six years, he's been in therapy with the same psychiatrist who recently bought a $1m yacht. Unemployed, and sitting alone in his apartment, 'Jack' is mildly autistic, extremely dull, self-loathing, and never read a novel or had romance in his life. The only woman who loves him is his divorced mother, whose hair is pink and neck tattooed. She gave 'Jack' her electric car, after she was convicted of drunk-driving. Like 'Jack,' the car pretends to be a vegan of sorts but is metaphorically a secret 'meat' eater, as it has to be charged on fossil fuel (gas) in order to run.

Most of the time, 'Jack' spends watching TV, where he has never seen a commercial with a white couple who are straight. He also views pornography and masturbates twice a day. Some evenings, he orders a coffee (made with fluoride water) and a vegan burger from his local takeaway. When it arrives, he takes his antidepressants and anxiety pills, then sips the coffee from a polystyrene cup.

He doesn't have to leave his apartment to buy a music disc, as he can avail of services like Spotify, YouTube Music or Apple Music, all at the push of a button. In fact, he doesn't have to speak to some store music buff, as he can get all this information from algorithms that recommend new artists and tracks.

Recently, he was recommended a Godless, diabolical song (about oral sex) by rapper Cardi B. After listening to it, 'Jack' smokes a cannabis joint, while downloading Zoom and chatting to 'friends' who he's never met face-to-face. He rarely leaves the house but, when he does go for a walk, he constantly films most things he sees—from a dog defecating in a park, to upskirt shots while travelling on a bus or train.

Before getting into bed, he takes a sleeping pill. The quilt on his bed has the rainbow pattern colours and, on his wall, hangs the Ukrainian flag upside-down. 'Jack' is also prone to suicidal thoughts. He lives in an age where the only thing safe to talk about is sports results; everything else is at risk of committing a 'thought crime.' All of this would surely bring a smile to the face of a demon.

The Irish writer John Waters, who is the antithesis of 'Jack,' has written a lot about music and culture. Growing up in the 1960s, he said that when he was a kid, and had albums or cassettes, he would take an armful or a pocket-full of them to a friend's house, and some other friends would gather around and listen to the music, with each person introducing the artist and talking about it.

He added: "Out of that kind of communion, expanded and multiplied many [...] times, was a living vibrant culture that was almost invisible in its generality. You were aware it was there, but you didn't see it until suddenly it erupted in the form of a new band. But when you think about it now, it's like 'push-button' stuff. So, if I want to send a song [to a friend], I just send you a link or whatever; you play it and might send me a two-line email saying, 'yea, that was great,' but you're not talking about what it's about."

The philosopher Hubert Dreyfus, during the 1980s' BBC TV series *The Great Philosophers*, said:

"We don't even seek truth anymore but simply efficiency. For us, everything is to be made as flexible as possible so as to be used as efficiently as possible."

Indeed, we seem to be reaching for an efficiency only to strive to become more efficient, thus ending up as slaves or soulless clones, as well as philistine vandals of high art.

In Colossians 3:23, St Paul said: 'Whatever you do, work at it with all your heart, as working for the Lord, not for human masters.' Paul is saying that if you work through the Lord, the outcome will be that derived of the Logos: Beauty, Logic, etc; whereas working for human masters at the altar of AI is open to errors or darkness.

Recently, a perceptive, discerning writer who will remain anonymous, said he asked AI to illustrate a self-portrait of what it looks like. The result was a grotesque-looking, smirking demon. Makes one wonder was the AI programmed by someone who was possessed by an evil spirit.

Chapter 10

"Is That All There Is?"

Did you know that there is a Peggy Lee song that unwittingly defines atheism? And that the song is allegedly Donald Trump's favourite? I'll come to that later, but first, I believe that no secularist *acts* as if atheism were true. Most 21st-century secular Humanists lead lives similarly moral to those who believe in God. But there is an enormous difference.

From a Christian perspective, the foundations for objective moral values and duties are anchored in God and can be justified. For atheists, there are no objective foundations for morality and no objective justification for having morals in a purely amoral universe filled with atoms bumping into one another. On atheism, righteous indignation is nothing more than a hairless monkey screeching.

On Naturalism (materialism), if there is such a thing as a distorted prototype of 'the self,' values and morality among such creatures are subjective or arbitrary shared beliefs in what is 'right' or 'wrong' or what functions best in certain situations. And most of these beliefs for Humanist-atheists, not all, are in some ways similar to the theistic worldview on morality, albeit a kind of borrowed morality for the atheist, piggy-backing on the residue of Christianity.

More: In a godless universe, love, self-sacrifice, friendship, relationships, procreation, art and literature, etc., are nothing more than relatively subjective illusions to pass the time and avoid boredom with no ultimate purpose or objective meaning. Such a situation is captured to a tee in Samuel Beckett's play *Waiting for Godot*, where the main characters struggle with boredom and meaninglessness, as they wait in vain for a friend who never arrives.

If the amoral universe really is just a brute fact, which is scientifically and theistically absurd, then the atheist's worldview is unliveable unless he or she gets psychologically 'creative' or is deluded. In such a Godless world, streets and houses become geometric blocks and plains with cement-shaped objects of all shapes and sizes, void of aesthetics. The sound of Mozart's Requiem would be nothing more than the primate jungle auditory observations of an ape: Vibrations in the air hitting the outer ear then middle ear, transduced into nerve impulses, then...

well, the rest are vibrations, molecules, and sound-wave frequency. You'll never see a monkey crying at an opera when Madam Butterfly starts squeaking.

Even the literature and information we read occasionally would be nothing more than billions of black, meaningless squiggles on components derived from felled trees and/or computer software, and not in the sense of an English-speaking person reading Chinese, but in the sense of a spider walking across a page of *Hamlet*, experiencing the physical imagery but not its meaning.

Furthermore, without God, the labours of millions of carers and charity workers worldwide in soup kitchens, shelters for the homeless and the sick and dying, and overseas aid are devoid of all objective values and ultimate meaning. Without God, they would be mere temporary, vanity projects, as death ends at the grave and the universe goes from Big Bang to pathetic icy squeak. Without God, all our accomplishments would ultimately be undone when the sun eventually incinerates the Earth.

However, as mentioned above, if the atheist lives his or her life as an illusion, and not by a 'rational atheistic' worldview that descends into nihilism, is it possible to be a happy individual? Someone who understood the ramifications of atheism, Friedrich Nietzsche, was miserable beyond words and spent his final year insane lying in a bed.

The great Humanist-atheist philosophers of yesteryear acknowledged the hopeless despair that it brings. From Bertrand Russell to Jean-Paul Sartre and Albert Camus, they acknowledged that life without God might have transient, momentary meaning, but it is without ultimate meaning. Is the average atheist aware of the implications of this? And how did they come to the realisation that belief in God was delusional?

In his impressive book *A Secular Age* (2007), philosopher Charles Taylor writes about the West's current age of 'authenticity,' meaning an individualistic era in which people are encouraged to sort out and make meaning of their own lives. Using reason and experience to find God instilled a sense of intellectual autonomy that led some to abandon God altogether.

Taylor writes that, as a result of this, a so-called "nova effect has been intensified. We are now living in a spiritual super-nova, a kind of galloping pluralism on the spiritual plane." Paradoxically, that leads some of us back to communal worship (favoured by many Humanist-atheists and their various ceremonies) and to yearn for something more than the self-sufficient power of reason. Some long for ultimate meaning, and that longing may end with God. God is always breaking in, says Taylor, stepping through the immanent frame of secularism. But when 'secular' God makes his appearance, Taylor finds he sounds just like Peggy Lee, telling a story, then singing in the refrain chorus: "Is That All There Is?"

This bleak song, which Peggy sung in 1969, is arguably the most depressing song ever written. It was inspired by the 1896 story "Disillusionment" ("Enttäuschung") by Thomas Mann, and it was later made into a song written by American songwriting team Jerry Leiber and Mike Stoller during the 1960s.

The song sums up precisely the real meaning of secularism. It tells the story of a young girl and the disappointments she experiences throughout her life. Everything seems empty and tinged with the melancholy of all things done, despite not having done all things.

Finally, totally disillusioned and left with a broken heart when her first love leaves her, her last words confront a way out by suicide. But she says she is in no hurry for that ultimate disappointment, saying in her last breath: "Is that all there is?"

For if there is no God, and this universe is all there is, then it is only logical (if logic exists) to consider Peggy Lee's song and 'break out the booze and let's start dancing,' if that's all there is. But deep-down, billions of people know that that is not all there is. Even unbelievers seem to intuitively 'suffer' from some form of phantom God. For them, consider the following: Do you have an open mind on God's existence, or is your mind fully closed and impervious to reason and filled with a stubborn intellect pride? If you have an open mind, will you let your intellect lead the way to find out where it leads to? Is a meaningless world all there is?

According to John Ganz, writing in *Genius*, tapes released by the *New York Times*, which contain interviews by journalist Michael D'Antonio for his 2014 biography *The Truth About Trump*, The Donald said this about the song: "It's a great song. Because I've had these tremendous successes and then I'm off to the next one, because, it's like, 'Oh, is that all there is?' That's a great song actually. That's a very interesting song, especially sang by her, because she had such a troubled life."

To answer the character in Peggy Lee's song in a charitable way, but with a pinch of condescension: *Honey, get a grip on yourself and quit navel-gazing. Acedia occurs when one rejects the Logos. You're looking at the world through the lens of Aergia, the Greek goddess of sloth. In the sentiments of a Ralph McTell song, let me take you by the hand and lead you through the streets of Philly's Kensington, I'll show you something, that will make you change your mind. And give yourself to God. Then feel the sun in your eyes and the summer breeze on your face, and realise that God, who confers you with free will, also has a plan for your life. Not only are you special, you have the potential to be great, but only through God. However, I empathize with you regarding your trip to the circus. When I first saw a circus, I also asked: "Is that all there is to a circus? The clowns ain't funny and the lions, elephants and dancing bears wearing tutus are being put through Hell. But if there is no God, then I apologise, as you are right to ask, 'Is that all there is?' Without God, life is more absurd and meaningless than circus bears dancing in tutus. But don't just take my word on this. The world's most-famous atheist philosopher in the 20th century was Bertrand Russell. Regarding Naturalism and mean-*

ing, he said we are the product of causes which had no prevision of the end they were achieving; that our origin, our growth, our hopes and fears, our loves and beliefs, are but the outcome of accidental collocations of atoms. He added: 'All the inspiration, all the noonday brightness of human genius, are destined to extinction in the vast death of the solar system, and that the whole temple of Man's achievement must inevitably be buried beneath the debris of a universe in ruins.'"

One is tempted to ask: Why didn't Russell convert to believing in God? The answer is, Russell's reluctance to make a leap of faith, based on reason, was theoretically psychological, and not ontological. Same applies to the late atheist icon, Christopher Hitchens. In my opinion, they both wanted moral autonomy.

And consider what the highly distinguished atheist philosopher, Thomas Nagel, had to say on the fear of God existing: "I speak from experience, being strongly subject to this fear myself: I want atheism to be true and am made uneasy by the fact that some of the most intelligent and well-informed people I know are religious believers. It isn't just that I don't believe in God and, naturally, hope that

I'm right in my belief. It's that I hope there is no God! I don't want there to be a God; I don't want the universe to be like that. My guess is that this cosmic authority problem is not a rare condition and that it is responsible for much of the scientism and reductionism of our time...". (Ref: *The Last Word*, pp. 130–131, Oxford University Press, 1997.)

When your brave father saves you from a burning house, don't ask, "Is that all there is to a fire?" Thank God you have been saved.

Chapter 11

In Praise of Biblical Language
Metaphors in song and verse

There is nothing quite like metaphors or symbolism to bring a book to life, especially when used as a literary device in poetry or fiction. It is also essential in song lyrics. But before deconstructing theologically two famous songs by The Eagles for metaphors and meaning, consider the power of metaphor in verse, poems, etc.

Many adults are metaphorically challenged, while younger children can be confused by homonyms (same-sounding words with different meanings) and metonymy (figure of speech with something associated with something else).

A child hearing radio reports of *guerrilla* warfare can conjure up images of heavily armed, silverback apes with AK-47s searching the jungle for the enemy. And how many young children who grew up in the 1960s/'70s thought Scotland Yard was a small backyard with a shed, somewhere in Highlands, where policemen wearing kilts would meet for tea and biscuits? Or to hear someone say, 'he has *catholic* tastes in literature (broad, varied) and think of him as a religious man.'

But the language in the Bible is where most people who don't study Scripture go from being challenged to almost becoming illiterate. One example is a story from Genesis. For many atheists, the Garden of Eden is a soft target to mock Christianity, by saying it is literally about a naked man and woman, tempted by a talking snake, to eat a forbidden apple from a tree. However, the majority of theologians have a more sophisticated view of the poetic, figurative language in the Bible. Although they ultimately believe in the authenticity of the Genesis account, they also believe metaphor is used to communicate truth in the story, as well as symbolism (we'll come back to this later).

Another example of atheists *and* early Church fathers' confusion of biblical language is the story of Galileo, who was a devout Christian. During that time in the early-17th century, *members* of the then-Church interpreted the Bible on a geocentric system, which derived from Aristotle and Ptolemy. This influenced the theology of the early-Church fathers and was, during that period, the world view of the scientific establishment. But they failed to see that this view clashed with the teachings of the Bible, some of which are poetic in style, infused with metaphors, metonymy, similes, symbolism, etc.

Galileo was trying to show the Church members that the heliocentric system was more in line with how the universe works, as opposed to geocentricism, and not what Aristotle taught. However, Galileo was imprisoned for heresy but later pardoned by the Church, whose previous members took some of the biblical text literally, and not poetically. The Bible is not a science book; thus it describes things phenomenologically and poetically. And let's face it: during sunrise or sunset, no one describes such a beautiful experience as an earth tilt.

And there is much truth and meaning in symbolism and metaphor. If we take the example in recent times when dilettantes in the media and chattering classes perpetually mined metaphors in a famous poem called *The Second Coming* by William Butler Yeats (1856-1939). The opening lines to the poem are as follows:

Turning and turning in the widening gyre
The falcon cannot hear the falconer;

Things fall apart; the centre cannot hold;
Mere anarchy is loosed upon the world,
The blood-dimmed tide is loosed, and everywhere
The ceremony of innocence is drowned ...

This poem was written a few decades after the philosopher Friedrich Nietzsche declared 'God is Dead' (we know he didn't mean God is literally dead, as he didn't believe in such an entity). In light of that phrase, the 'falcon' can be interpreted as Mankind turning its back (not literally, of course) on the 'falconer,' God: *'Things fall apart/The centre cannot hold'*: objective morality collapses, as humans lose their moral compass; *'Mere anarchy is loosed upon the world/The blood-dimmed tide is loosed, and everywhere/The ceremony of innocence is drowned'*: moral chaos follows the death of God (The Great Wars, the decadence of the West, and conflicts in the East). Nietzsche said it first: by killing God, we unchain the earth from the sun and wipe away the horizon with a sponge. As for Yeats' poem: no one can deny, despite poetic language, that the metaphors in his masterpiece are eerily prophetic.

To return to Adam and Eve, the same can be said about the metaphors and symbolism in this story: the 'apple' on the tree is a metaphor for omnipotence, something only God can possess; the serpent is a symbol of evil or metaphor for the devil (literally, there is no 'talking snake' written about in Genesis 3:1; it seems like many atheists use the smear comparing it to the talking snake in Disney's *Jungle Book*.

When you think of it, the profound meaning and spiritual authenticity of this story is acted out every day in the world by human beings trying to be their own god and failing miserably. And the fallen state of the world, after Adam and Eve sinned, is testament to the flawed condition of Mankind, despite our greatness and uniqueness.

Then there are the metaphors in Isaiah 64:8: 'But now, O Lord, You are our Father, We are the clay, and You our Potter, and all of us are the work of Your hand.' As well as the Lord being our 'Potter,' He's also referred to as being our Shepperd (Psalms 23:1; Ezekiel 34). For a child, this metaphor can conjure an image of a tall, bearded man in a meadow, dressed in robes, surrounded by sheep, while holding up a long staff.

And when Jesus said 'I am the door' and 'the bread of life' (John 10:7 and 6:35), well, that's bound to confuse any youngster; while in Revelations 21:6: 'I am Alpha and Omega, the beginning and the end' (a paradox sounding like quantum physics). However, in this great book of truth and wisdom, there are so many stories with a spiritual dimension that can be *partially* understood metaphorically. In the story of Noah's Ark (a baptism, renewal, or cleansing of Mankind), the chaos emerging from disharmony with the Creator is poetically represented by the primordial waters falling from the sky," according to Christopher Kaczor, professor of philosophy at Loyola Marymount University, L.A.

He adds: "The story of the Flood, in other words, is not a tale of God becoming frustrated and lashing out at human beings. The flood represents the consequences of disharmony with God. In acting out of harmony with Divine Love, we cause primordial chaos within ourselves. When we act against our ideals, we create within ourselves an inner schizophrenia. We pit the best of ourselves against the rest of ourselves."

But aside from metaphors and a spiritual dimension, most theologians believe there was a great universal flood, and the fossil record is remarkably consistent with the biblical account of Noah's era.

In the case of the Prodigal Son (Mankind) and his Father (God) who forgives and welcomes 'home' the genuinely remorseful son seeking redemption, we have a perfect parable rich in metaphor, love, hope and forgiveness.

And what to make of Jonah 'entombed' in the whale? Another apt metaphor foreshadowing the death and resurrection of Jesus on the third day. But it's not just Christians who appreciate the rich language and metaphors of the Bible. The late atheist writer Christopher Hitchens once paid tribute to the King James version of the Bible, as did his friend, biologist Richard Dawkins.

Back in 2011, during the 400th anniversary of the translation, the two most famous atheists in the world expressed appreciation for the Bible's contribution to English literature. In an article in *Vanity Fair*, Hitchens wrote: "Though I am sometimes reluctant to admit it, there really is something 'timeless' in the Tyndale/King James synthesis. For generations, it provided a common stock of references and allusions, rivalled only by Shakespeare in this respect. It resounded in the minds and memories of literate people, as well as of those who acquired it only by listening."

During his time battling cancer, this quote by Hitchens contradicts the sub-title of one of his books, *God Is Not Great (How Religion Poisons Everything)*. However, he relented when it came to honouring the King James Bible, which was first published in 1611.

In an article in *The Christian Post*, Audrey Barrick wrote: "But the bestselling author went further to criticize other translations of the Bible and ongoing attempts to update it. Offering one comparison, Hitchens cited a passage in the New Testament book of Philippians, which he read at his father's funeral: 'Finally, brethren, whatsoever things are true, whatsoever things are honest, whatsoever things are just, whatsoever things are pure, whatsoever things are lovely, whatsoever things are of good report; if there be any virtue, and if there be any praise, think on these things.' (King James Version)

Amid numerous Bible translations and customized Scriptures, Hitchens lamented the gradual eclipse of the King James Bible, according to Audrey Barrick, quoting Hitchens again: "A culture that does not possess this common store of image and allegory will be a perilously thin one. To seek restlessly to update it or make it 'relevant' is to miss the point, like yearning for a hip-hop Shakespeare," he wrote. "'Man is born unto trouble as the sparks fly upward,' says the Book of Job. Want to try to improve that for Twitter?"

A year later in 2012, Richard Dawkins said he supported the Department for Education's drive (by the then secretary, Michael Gove) to make sure every public school in the nation has a copy of the King James Bible. "A native speaker of English who has never read a word of the King James Bible is verging on the barbarian," said Dawkins in a column for *The Guardian.* Despite remaining a non-believer, the biologist said he would have donated to the cause had he been given the opportunity to do so.

But it's not just metaphors that are used to convey truth in the King James version. The Bible also uses poetry, hyperbole, didactic teaching, and much more. An example of phenomenological language can be found in in the Book of Joshua (10:27): "But at the time of the going down of the sun, Joshua commanded, and they took them down from the trees and threw them into the cave where they had hidden themselves, and they set large stones against the mouth of the cave, which remain to this very day." "Sunset" here doesn't mean that the sun "went down" scientifically.

Then there are the biblical passages about trees and rivers that clap their hands, and mountains that burst into song; metaphors about how creation inspires people to praise God. Or, according to author Ruth M. Bancewicz, does the non-human creation actually worship God in some unconscious way? Writing in *Science and Belief*, she said: "This is the question that Mark Harris, lecturer in Science and Religion at Edinburgh University, asked in his seminar at the Faraday Institute earlier this year. This is particularly relevant to the current series of posts on how a scientist's faith is enhanced through their own work."

Bancewicz said Verse 12 of Isaiah 55 is a good example of these natural praise texts. 'You will go out in joy and be led forth in peace; the mountains and hills will burst into song before you, and all the trees of the field will clap their hands.' "The writer of Psalm 19 was more cautious, saying that although 'there is no speech', the heavens still 'declare the glory of God'. Many of these passages are either songs or invitations to praise God. They might also be pointing to some great work God will do in the future or a testimony of what he has done in the past."

As for metaphors and meaning in popular songs, consider the giant rock anthem from 1976 by American group The Eagles, "Hotel California," the lyrics of which could be interpreted to mean an invitation to praise the Prince of Darkness, not to mention 'taking the ticket' (Faustian Pact).

Ostensibly, the song is about a man travelling in a strange rural setting out Westcoast of America, unsure about his surroundings. It is composed and written by band members Don Felder, Don Henley, and Glen Frey.

On his journey, the protagonist encounters themes of excess, disillusionments, and the dark side of the American Dream, infused with the sins of hedonism, temptation, and mendacity. The following speculates hypothetically on possible metaphors behind the enigmatic narrative. The hotel represents a 'Hollywood' state of mind; a place marinated in spiritual decay. On arrival in such a decadent Babylon of the West, the protagonist enters its cryptic prison gates, lured in by the 'warm smell of colitas' (slang for marijuana) and the 'pretty-pretty boys' who are 'all prisoners here of our own device,' trapped behind the giant gates in a Hell of their own making. Jesus said: "Enter through the narrow gate. For wide is the gate and broad is the road that leads to destruction, and many enter through it. But small is the gate and narrow the road that leads to life, and only a few find it." (Matthew 7:13-14)

In "Hotel California," the dark underbelly of the rock'n'roll lifestyle is laid bare in such metaphors and symbolism; a lifestyle that promises glamour, fame, and fortune, but instead delivers emptiness, loneliness, and the superficial ugliness of 'Tinseltown' trash.

But turning one's back in the lifestyle in this place is *almost* impossible. 'You can check out anytime you like, but you can never leave.' In such a place, addiction and degenerate behaviour enslave the 'guests.'

The Eagles had other songs with interesting theological themes, but apart from "Hotel California," another one of them stands out: "Take It To The Limit" (1975).

The founding members of The Eagles, Don Henley and Glenn Frey, wrote this song, along with fellow musician Randy Meisner, who sang the song.

Meisner had struggled with addiction and depression throughout his life, and as Eagles' success grew, he found himself increasingly overwhelmed by the pressures of fame. He drew inspiration for "Take It To The Limit" from his own experiences of pushing himself to the brink in pursuit of his dreams.

Using a highway as a metaphor for one's journey in life, many have interpreted the song to mean overcoming fear and doubt in order to pursue one's dreams by pushing oneself to his or her limits. The song opens with the following lyrics:

All alone at the end of the evening
And the bright lights have faded to blue
I was thinking 'bout a woman who might have
    loved me And I never knew."

The protagonist reflects on his life and laments on lost love. He also says:

And when you're looking for your freedom
Nobody seems to care
And you can't find the door
Can't find it anywhere

When there's nothing to believe in
Still you're coming back, you're running back
You're coming back for more

The Godless sentiment of the above verse is the existential moral maze many of us find ourselves in today's world, which is far more decadent than 1970s' America and beyond where finding one's freedoms is an uphill battle.

Epilogue

Throughout this book, I have endeavoured to deconstruct, thus, highlight speculations on the narratives and lyrics of some of the world's most popular songs of the 20th and 21st centuries. The reason I did not select Hymns, Psalms, or other classic styles of music in that genre is because the messages are theologically overt. Better, I thought, to deconstruct the subtext of hidden theological meaning behind the music genres of Ballads, Rock'n'Roll, Soul, and Pop.

I have shown that, theologically, songs and all Art would be meaningless in a universe composed solely of atoms and random events. Brains do not write songs, but minds do with the help of the machine-brain inside our physical skull. The lyrics contained in the thoughts of songwriters emanate from the soulful sentiments of the Mind. And just like the soul is non-physical, so too are our desires, dreams, loves, hates, believes et al. None of these can be measured, weighed, or examined in a lab. Their existence debunks cold, amoral Naturalism. There is nowhere in the brain that neuroscientists could point to and say: 'Oh, look, there's the part where she's saddened by the melody and lyrics in "The Sun Ain't Gonna Shine Anymore." During such a song under lab observation, a neuroscientist will only see electrical circuit flashing and waves emanating from a grey chunk of wrinkled fat, unlike the Mind that contains immaterial, mental states and a soul.

Many songs are filled with love, hate, beauty, desires, and beliefs, inspired by thoughts that are not electrochemical reactions in the brain. And I believe that most atheists feel the same way, at least about love and beauty.

Regarding Logos: I endeavoured to show how the one, true meaning of life points to Christ Jesus on The Cross. Although many atheists and other non-Christian religious can lead decent lives and act logically and kind, it is difficult for them to justify their actions as morally good and rationally compatible with their world view, especially in song, as illustrated in "The Sun Ain't Gonna Shine Anymore," the meaning of which would be reduced to the extinguishment of nuclear fusion. In such a world, Naturalism can't present an adequate account of love. Scientifically/biologically, such behaviour is the result of atoms bumping into one another in the brain of an evolved, hairless ape who screeches. And what ape would crave another creature's affections—or sing about them so passionately, for that matter?

To repeat an extract from the chapter on sin and idolatry: If God's creation is reduced to Darwinian, Naturalistic grammar: The lyrics of the song's chorus would read something like this: *"The nuclear fusion aint' gonna radiate light anymore/The earth's natural satellite aint gonna rise in the celestial sphere/The secreted liquid from lacrimal glands are always aerosoling your visual organs/When you're without a chemical reaction in the brain."*

Doesn't have the same romantic ring to it, does it? See original lyrics below in brackets.

(The sun ain't gonna shine anymore
The moon ain't gonna rise in the sky
The tears are always clouding your eyes
When you're without love)

In conclusion, the next time you hear a song, consider the meaning of its lyrics or melody and the theological implications. In 1966, a TV advert featured a man smoking a cigar called Hamlet to the tune of Bach's "Air on G String." The following year, the band Procol Harum used that Bach-inspired melody in part of their classic song, "A Whiter Shade of Pale." In lyrics or melody, sometimes 'a cigar is not a cigar'.